primal sanities!
a Tribute to Walt Whitman
an Anthology of Poems and Essays

primal sanities!
a Tribute to Walt Whitman
an Anthology of Poems and Essays

edited by Mankh (Walter E. Harris III)
and George Wallace

Allbook Books
Selden, NY, USA

© 2007 by Walter E. Harris III.
All rights reserved.
Except for the quoting of brief passages the text and individual poems
may not be reproduced in any manner for publication, electronic or otherwise,
without the written permission of the publisher.

For each contributor, all rights for his/her essays and/or poems revert to the
individual artist (or his/her publisher as per previous arrangements).

Cover photo:
427882: Anonymous. *Daguerreotype portrait of Walt Whitman*. circa, 1853.
Daguerreotype. Rare Books Division, The New York Public Library, Astor, Lenox
and Tilden Foundations.

Jean Franco's "Foreword to the *Countersong*" and excerpts from Pedro Mir's
*Countersong to Walt Whitma*n are reprinted with the permission of the publisher
<www.azuleditions.com>, Jean Franco, and translator Jonathan Cohen.

Used by permission of Council Oak Books, *Native New Yorkers:*
The Legacy of the Algonquin People of New York © 2002 by Evan T. Pritchard,
quotes from pages 305, 314, 465.

Printed on recycled paper (30% post consumer)
in the United States of America.

Published by: Allbook Books
　　　　　　　PO Box 562
　　　　　　　Selden, NY 11784
　　　　　　　www.allbook-books.com

ISBN-10: 0-9743603-6-8
ISBN-13: 978-0-9743603-6-2

give me again O Nature your primal sanities!

> ~ Walt Whitman
> from "Give Me the Splendid Silent Sun"

for Aunt Barbara
1928 - 2007

with much thanks
for the encouragement,
and with loving memories

*

a ribbon of blue sky is a trail of your love . . .

thanks to . . .

Annabelle Moseley ~ for assistance with the poetry selection process.

Barbara Reiher-Meyers ~ for E-mailing a submissions notice to poets.

Barbara Harris ~ for artistic input and encouragement.

Buffalo ~ for discussion and ideas about Whitman and Sewanacky. And for revealing the fact that the Sun sings too!

J R (Judy) Turek ~ for editorial and many other comments on the manuscript.

Richard Savadsky ~ for encouragement.

Singh-Kaur ~ for helping to keep the space comfy.

All the contributors!!!!!

Lisa Vasher ~ for her phone-side manner.

The price-quote, pre-flight, and printing crew ~ for making the book 3-D.

The trucker who delivered the books, the waitress who made the coffee that kept the trucker going . . .

& Whitman for reminding us of almost everything.

The name

Allbook Books

**honors Uncle Alan
who was a kind man and a lover of books**

contents

	page
foreword	13
poems	
Preface for Walt Whitman ~ D.H. Melhem	19
Walt and the Quaker Woman ~ Vince Clemente	20
Walt ~ Geraldine Green	21
"¡O, Walt Whitman de barba sensitiva . . ." ~ Pedro Mir	22
Translation ~ Jonathan Cohen	23
" "¡Poetas venidos... " " ~ Pedro Mir	24
Translation ~ Jonathan Cohen	25
Whitman Recidivist ~ Gary Corseri	26
or a stone to keep your world small ~ Edgar Carlson	28
Go Like Whitman ~ George Wallace	29
In All Things ~ Mindy Kronenberg	30
Circuit ~ Christina M. Rau	31
The Material Poet ~ Pramila Venkateswaran	32
Earth Drunk ~ Ernie Wormwood	33
press my foot to the earth ~ Sasha Ettinger	34
Paumanok: Early Morning ~ Vince Clemente	35
Visiting With Walt ~ Jeanette Klimszewski	36
A Walk in the River ~ Andrea Rowen	38
On a Rainy Day, If Whitman Went to the Mall ~ Mankh	40
Searching for Absolutes ~ David B. Axelrod	41
Looking for Walt Whitman at C.W. Post ~ Norbert Krapf	42
Whitman's Photograph Speaks ~ Gladys Henderson	44
The Voice in Wind and Waves ~ Robert Savino	45
Into the Light: Safe Haven 1944 ~ Ruth Sabath Rosenthal	46
Poets Gone ~ Ray Freed	48
Walt Whitman Among the Reaching Hands ~ Martin Willitts, Jr.	50
O how shall I warble myself for the dead one I loved?	51
~ Maxwell Corydon Wheat, Jr.	
"Walt, you are my gestalt..." ~ Darrel Blaine Ford	53
Unfinished Story ~ Evelyn Kandel	54
A Love Song for Walt Whitman's Mother ~ Annabelle Moseley	56
Walking My Open Road ~ Tammy Nuzzo-Morgan	58
"fish-shape Paumanok" ~ Mankh	60
The Walt Whitman Birthplace ~ Alan Semerdjian	61
Walt Whitman's Daughters ~ Norbert Krapf	62
Father of Us All ~ Charlene Babb Knadle	64
Beyond the palisade ~ Ann Kenna	65
Writing Helps ~ Mark Donnelly	66
Ode to a Dandelion ~ Muriel Harris Weinstein	68
Stranded at the Walt Whitman Mall ~ Barbara Southard	70

page

Autumn (just about a mile from the Mall) ~ Anthony Policano	71
Walt and the Wheelbarrow of Poetry ~ Martin Willitts, Jr.	72
Flying Island ~ Richard Savadsky	74
End of Day ~ J R Turek	75
Walt Whitman: "Of Life immense in passion, pulse, and power . . ." ~ Genevieve Shore	76
Watching the Stars Go By ~ Rita Katz	78
Walt Whitman Was a River (#489) ~ Douglas G. Swezey	79
New Hymns for the Promised Land ~ Andrea Rowen	82
Song for Walt Whitman ~ George Wallace	84

essays

excerpts from "Paumanok, and My Life On It As Child and Young Man" ~ Walt Whitman	89
Starting From Sewanacky ~ Mankh	90
Foreword to the *Countersong* ~ Jean Franco	92
Joint Tenants In Reality ~ Tammy Nuzzo-Morgan	94
A Forward Glance Towards Roads Un-traveled ~ Annabelle Moseley	97
The Colors of Long Island ~ Annabelle Moseley	99
Telegram From Walt Whitman: The Long and Immense Road STOP Sing! STOP Be Free ~ Mankh	100
Holding Each Other's Hands ~ Geraldine Green	106
Walt Whitman's Natural Resources ~ Maxwell Corydon Wheat, Jr.	109
Poets to Come: Teaching Whitman in High School ~ Bill Zavatsky	113
Shopping for Inspiration ~ Ali Lebow	123
Virginia Tech and Our Need for a Poetic Language of Mourning ~ Maxwell Corydon Wheat, Jr.	124

bios	130
acknowledgments	142
Allbook Books info.	143

foreword

Love Letters

This anthology came about from one of many "...letters from God dropt in the street ..." as Walt Whitman wrote (though at that time he was perhaps attempting to convey to an often thick-headed humanity how easy it really is to actually find God in whatever form suits your fancy).

And noticing the letter, I picked it up-- a bit hesitant at first because one doesn't always pick stuff up off the street, but you see, it had Whitman's name on it, and for all he has added to my life, I owed him the favor.

After dusting off the letter and opening it up... I began to discover all sorts of writings and people who had been, and still are, inspired by America's ol' grey-bearded bard. And when it comes to "made in America," I prefer to think of Walt Whitman or Mark Twain or the hundreds and hundreds of American Indian tribes and native peoples, rather than apple pies (which I enjoy) or a military-industrial-corporate-complex with destructive habits (which I disdain).

I say no land or people or circumstances ever existed so needing a race of singers and poems differing from all others, and rigidly their own, as the land and people and circumstances of our United States need such singers and poems to-day, and for the future.
             from "A Backward Glance O'er Travel'd Roads"

Whitman is also quoted as writing: the true job of the poet is to "cheer up slaves, and horrify despots," (to which I take the liberty to update-- *liberate* slaves).

As to the letter "God dropt"... I was at a party talking with a few other poets and I happened to say: "So many Long Island poets write poems about Whitman, there's probably enough for a book"... and the little clock on the table chimed three!

Being a noticer of signs, I thought: 'that's interesting... but anyway it's a nice afternoon and I have better things to do with my time than put together an anthology, what with all the correspondences and decisions and people to deal with.'

So I had another glass of wine and chatted up the party for a while until... a friend and fellow-poet walks up and hands me a copy of *Song of Myself* (which I was already familiar with) -- signed not by Whitman but by numerous friends, fellow poets, and people I had not even met -- as a kind of appreciation for my previous poetic efforts. (By the way, Whitman's "myself" is as much "him" as it is a voice for all the little "selfs" who comprise the cosmic "Self".)

I was deeply touched by this gift but my facial expression was a wince (confirmed by another friend who saw me) because I knew then that (remember the clock chiming three?) the Universe was prodding me to put together this book and though reluctant, who am I to say "no" to the Universe?

So I shook the dust off my tired shoulders and convinced "myself" that this would actually be fun, "Afoot and light-hearted I take to the open road..." or computer, as the case may be. (You can find an inspiring quote, on nearly every page of *Leaves of Grass* even if you open it at random.)

Thankfully, co-editor, George Wallace (being a Whitman fan and aficionado) gladly came along for the ride, and others who helped along the open road, and of course the wonderful and talented writers whose work graces these pages.

What you are holding now is actually a bunch of "letters," love letters, disguised as poems and essays for, to, about, referencing, riffing off of, contemplating, mimicking, attempting to define, embrace, even call to task, and otherwise sit down and have a meal and a drink with... Walt Whitman.

...give me comrades and lovers by the thousand!

Well, you got 'em, Walt, though whether in the form you really wanted I could not be sure.

In any case, the poems and essays herein aim to give the individual, as well as the world-at-large, a taste of what Whitman called for with an exclamation point: *primal sanities!*

~ Mankh (Walter E. Harris III)
July 2007

poems

O take my hand Walt Whitman!
Such gliding wonders! such sights and sounds!
Such join'd unended links, each hook'd to the next,
Each answering all, each sharing the earth with all.

~ Walt Whitman
from "Salut au Monde!"

Preface for Walt Whitman

One's-self I sing, a simple separate person,
Yet utter the word Democratic, the word En-Masse.

Poem of my life
from you I extrapolate a country
as your particles assemble and cohere
on my palette of rainbow mountains
that range a geography of waste images
to compose
a simple, separate person
who has dreamed America
a long, hard time . . .

~ D.H. Melhem

Walt and the Quaker Woman

Walt, I feel thee is right,
he whispered to Horace, recalling
the Quaker woman who blessed him,
anointed him along his forehead
with her thumb.

And again, *I could not tell thee,*
but I think thee is right,
the end-of-day light
skittering cloud-cover
along the fissures
of his face.
But why now, this voice
out of shore reeds, older
than a cicada's song?

Yet Horace understood
said nothing, read
the shine in the old man's face.
And that evening, before leaving,
he kissed him on the forehead
the way a son honors a father,
the way....

But we know, how for Walt
memory is a fishhook
trapped in a kelp-bed,
blunted yet fierce enough
to haul in a blue
fighting for its life,
still dreaming the Sound's deep waters, there,
far beyond the mudflats.

~ Vince Clemente

poet's note:
Before Whitman's passing he told Horace Traubel - writer, editor, and friend - of his memory of being anointed when he was three-and-a-half years old. Another powerful memory for Whitman was of apple orchards.

Walt

you with your jaunty smile and eyes in a teacup
you with your hat on one side a wide brimmed smile blowing over the
                                                                         hempsteads
you with your blackthorn stick and stride your billowing voice
                                            lamenting the parting of seabirds
you with your arms like happy windmills! waving to the sea the land
the railroads and soldiers
you with your laughing beard like zeus baring his chest as you make
your way round the boundaries of oceans
you, walt whitman of the long line and bounding somersaults of tender
                                                                                 poetry
walt with your working man's hands and mystery in the digging of
graves and gardens and planting of trees
here on your beloved paumanok fishtailed island
in your heart of lobsters and clams dancing
inside your wonderful beard the king james bible walking
with each step you make as you mark the bounds
stopping to stroke a dog, touch a child
smiling as you see someone you resemble
a woman holding a child, an old man a prophet a drugstore owner

you walt, pray to the sea and the air as i pray
bending your knees to better understand the blades of grass

   ~ Geraldine Green

From *Countersong to Walt Whitman*

¡O, Walt Whitman de barba sensitiva
era una red al viento!
Vibrada y se llenaba de encendidas figuras
de novia y donceles, de bravos y labriegos,
de rudos mozalbetes camino del riachuelo,
de guapos con espuelas y mozas con sonrisa,
de marchas presurosas de seres infinitos,
de trenzas o sombreros . . .
Y tu fuiste escuchado
camino por camino
golpeándoles el pecho
palabra con palabra.
¡O, Walt Whitman de barba candorosa,
alcanzo por los años tu ropa llamarada!

~ Pedro Mir

O Walt Whitman, your sensitive beard
was a net in the wind!
It throbbed and filled with ardent figures
of sweethearts and youths, of brave souls and farmers,
of country boys walking to creeks,
of rowdies wearing spurs and maidens wearing smiles,
of the hurried marches of numberless beings,
of tresses or hats . . .
And you went on listening
road after road,
striking their heartstrings
word after word.
O Walt Whitman of guileless beard,
I have come through the years to your red blaze of fire!

~ Translation by Jonathan Cohen

From *Countersong to Walt Whitman*

"¡Poetas venidos, levantaos, porque vosotros debéis justificarme!"
Aquí estamos, Walt Whitman, para justificarte.
Aquí estamos
        por ti
                pidiendo paz.
La paz que requieras
para empujar el mundo con tu canto.
Aquí estamos
        salvando tus colinas de Vermont,
tus selvas de Maine, el zumo y la fragancia de tu tierra,
tus guapos con espuelas, tus mazas con sonrisas,
tus rudos mozalbetes camino del riachuelo.
Salvándolos, Walt Whitman, de los traficantes
que toman tu lenguaje por lenguaje de guerra.
¡No, Walt Whitman, aquí están los poetas de hoy,
los obreros de hoy, los pioneros de hoy, los campesinos
de hoy,
       firmes y levantados para justificarte!
¡Oh, Walt Whitman de barba levantada!
Aquí estamos sin barba,
sin brazos, sin oídos,
sin fuerzas en los labios,
mirando de reojo,
rojo y perseguidos,
llenos de pupilas
que a través de las islas se dilatan,
llenos de coraje, de nudos de soberbia
que a través de los pueblos se desatan,
con tu signo y tu idioma de Walt Whitman
aquí estamos
        en pie
                para justificarte,
¡continuo compañero
de Manhattan!

~ Pedro Mir

"Poets to come! . . . Arouse! for you must justify me."
Here we are, Walt Whitman, to justify you.
Here we are
        for your sake
                demanding peace.
The peace you needed
to drive the world with your song.
Here we are
        saving your hills of Vermont,
your woods of Maine, the sap and fragrance of your land,
your spurred rowdies, your smiling maidens,
your country boys walking to creeks.
Saving them, Walt Whitman, from the tycoons
who take your language for the language of war.
No, Walt Whitman, here are the poets of today,
the workers of today, the pioneers of today, the peasants of today,
        firm and roused to justify you!
O Walt Whitman of aroused beard!
Here we are without beards,
without arms, without ears,
without any strength in our lips,
spied on,
red and persecuted,
full of eyes
wide open throughout the islands,
full of courage, of knots of pride
untied through all the nations,
with your sign and your language, Walt Whitman,
here we are
        standing up
                to justify you
our constant companion
of Manhattan!

~ Translation by Jonathan Cohen

Whitman Recidivist

I know I am restless and make others so...
 For I confront peace, security, and all the settled laws,
  to unsettle them...

Walt Whitman can't remember
what he did with America.
It was there in his back pocket
yesterday or the day before:
caroling, brawling, lusty, democratic;
stretching its broadbacked plains
in the sun between seas.
He walks from door to door
selling subscriptions to the Universe.
Who are these sad-eyed does,
this tamed race, moping proletariat?
What are these buildings
yeasting on the plains,
that drone of the cities—
ennui echoing ennui?
Men on the moon, rockets,
telethis and telethat—
but what Vision?—
all the wires entangling:
some hydra-headed nullifidian
sucking the wounds of the eyes,
eating democracy, spitting it out—
these people this land
lost   O   lost   lost.

Walt Whitman decides to invent
America anew—
towering architecture, spires,
cathedrals of the common man,
with the fierce light of the free heart bursting,
spinning the golden spinnakers—
manly exteriors,
soft feminine contours inside—
fit for the forest and prairie,
taking its proper name from them—
revealed in the splendor of mountains.

He needs no Constitution.
He needs no legal shenanigans.
Give it back to the Indians who nourished it!
Give it back to the Blacks who bled for it!
Give it back to the Mexicanos
who owned it first.
Give it back to the Chinese
who laid the tracks
over their dead bodies.

Unraveling, evolving, manifesting,
touching the planets and stars,
white beard pointed jauntily to Orion,
loins resting languorously
against the hot flanks of Alpha Centauri…

Raging, laughing, crying, decrying;
prodding, urging, discommoding, incanting;
demonic mandarin, mage, magellanic—
hurtling humongous challenges again:

Where is the nation that can contain him?
Where are the people to sunder their shrines?

~ Gary Corseri

or a stone to keep your world small
a stone to amputate scotland
or a semipermeable stone
a fence to let money in a fence to let money out
a latticework of fixed lances all pointed south
a stone to fence out ocelots and coyotes and the
    silent H in hombre
a fence to re-disenfranchise a young man trimming lauraceous
    shrubbery in suffolk county
a fence around a mosque in brooklyn with No Parking signs all
    down this side of the street and down along their side also.
charlene, the oculus is a centerpiece painted into a corner
hadrian is the hearthhole he is intersection and cloverleaf
he is whitman he is blue bull and iberian owl and a leaf of grass
    in courtship dance
this is where boys perform like swallows
this is where a mediolanum redhead put a mockingbird on
    the emperor's finger
this is where a redhead danced like a bluebird with a scorpion's
    stinger

    ~ Edgar Carlson

Go Like Walt Whitman

sometimes i wonder why it feels like i am the only sunny day i know
anyhow this is america, all the bright day long
    dogwoods unravel before my eyes
bees like yo-yo trees attack the sun, there are peepers down at the pond
someone wearing black clothes is comforting someone
like a frog quoting scripture near an old rock
when a nation has dirty hands it smears everything it touches
when a nation is up all night it gets cranky
it will feed on anything it can find
including the appetites of the weak
sometimes a president will get out of hand and blame it on the weather
the clouds have exceptional needs, he says
the rainfall is exceptionally dangerous
this is some country! a ruffian with unwarranted powers
sometimes it will plant peace into the brains of the people
    like yellow roses
other times it will plant you face first into the window box of war
america, just because it is possible to sail your big red barn through
    the neighbor's living room
that does not mean it is right or proper to do so
when i see you misbehave like this, america
i want to go like walt whitman
i want to roar like angels out of your tonsorial dawn

  ~ George Wallace

In All Things

All truths wait in all things.
   ~ Walt Whitman

Holding your weathered covers in my hand
I await the greatness that arises from words,
a handful of beads broken from their leash
sprawled on the page to glitter in my sight.

How you unraveled the benediction
of *The damp in the night*, what surges and seethes
beneath conventional speech; I collect your words
like shells sprawled on a deserted beach,

coins fallen from pockets to clatter on stone.
I follow their pattern like leaves strewn
on a furry lawn, the small pointed palms
and stems caught mid-dance on the blades.

I followed the footprints in sand and grass,
witnessed the beautiful, bathing young men,
the curious spinster, the pensive old soldier,
the Black horseman resting his reins in the shade.

I feel the swell and sway of your voice
in the raucous chatter of birds, the wood-drake
and the mockingbird, the goose and the
wood-duck, rousing the winged spirit

from within. Even in those moments
when the world's pockets seemed empty
and bereft of gifts, I held your tattered text
in my hands, opened the split binding

to wherever the heft of pages found me,
and knew, in the alchemy of your poems
I would find all things, my private treasure,
and I would never feel alone.

   ~ Mindy Kronenberg

Circuit

Mouth, tongue, lips, teeth, roof of the mouth, jaws, and the jaw-hinges...
            from "I Sing the Body Electric" ~ Walt Whitman

The veins connect, electric,
As do lungs, hips, front teeth,
Conducting a magnetic wave
Up, out, and back down
Through birthmarks and abrasions,
Mapped out of scar tissue. Lymph
Nodes quiver against
Glands, hands, feet,
Under shock, impulses that
Leap across synapses in the skull,
Along the jaw line,
Ending with a grin.

~ Christina M. Rau

The Material Poet

Walt, you materialist rolling naked in the tall grasses of Long Island,
rejoicing that a mall is named after you; its razzle-dazzle,
its silks, cottons, wood, foam, wax, granite, fluff, metal, glass,
the relax-a-beds and massage chairs, wonder bras and plunge necklines,
these things of the earth, shaped by the mind and cast
back in the mall behind glass and luminous walls to excite,
nature recast by human urge to recreate, break, renew.

Home, resort, bridge, garden, school, borough, or award
could bear your name and you would be cool about it, for
these are all things of this world within which beat human hearts
whose rhythms you listened to and joy rose to your lips and eyes.

How you believed in the world as fruit!
If we believed only the seed mattered
and threw out the flesh, the fruit would lose its name!

~ Pramila Venkateswaran

Earth Drunk

This morning with clouds moving in grey sky miles
over the houses across the street, I pull tall grass from
under the back yard stoop and a chunk of dirt comes up,
so I shake it to get the dirt off the weed, let it fall
back to the earth, the wheat from the chaff, and as its
farmy earthy perfume seduces my brain, I remember
who I am:

a woman who dislikes blacktop and chainlink
a child of rivers who jumps from wharves not piers
a farmgirl who loves her father still more than anyone else, bound
       by something that has no real name, a kind of light or jazz or
       electricity, or Beethoven's Fifth
a mother who loves all her children as if each is the only one
       and trembles at the risks they take and the horrible new fear
       of surviving them
a citizen of the world like Charlie Chaplin
a friend flawed by what other friends have done to me, for me
a sister of two brothers with troubles and a tall girl named Anna
a caretaker of others, plower of fields, cousin to many
a mower of lawns, teacher of willing and unwilling students
a Castaneda clown, pliant piano player, dog lover, baseball-
    opera buff, non-diving driver, peaceophile,
      a messenger for all this, not even sure what to say, or how or
                                            with what
      (what if I am in the wrong medium?)
      with paint or lead or keys or blood or blocks of letters that say
                                                    wormwood
    on the kitchen counter, then girl, then ?????
a writer of words trying to make a message, a poem
    in Sherman Alexie smoke, in Faulkner nakedness
to be gripped in some kind of genesis, put out grass and grow, grow
                                                           grass
      inside of me, let it peek out of my eyes and ears, sneak out from
                                                             my teeth,
all caused by the lilt of some dirt I am shaking back to where it came
                                                                    from,
      to where it belongs in the world, is there anything so perfect?
all the while swooning from the drunkenness of just how good it smells.

~ Ernie Wormwood

press my foot to the earth
~ Walt Whitman

i "press my foot to the earth"
playfully pocket rocks and
wayward leaves
hues of
strawberry lemon tangerine
i finger lacy fern
bunched in mossy damp
collect secrets of reckless acorns
bound to become oaks
whistle with the whistling trees
jostled by uninvited wind

before light fades and
wild darkness takes hold
waning sun
still generous
warms my pale features
bone-like torso
narrow shoulders
i inhale dusk tinged air
inhale the untidy serenity
of a forest cathedral

~ Sasha Ettinger

Paumanok: Early Morning

This first blush:
 shedding of grayself
  for color of iris, of lilac rain.

The Island
 turns to the sun
  breaking its hymen.

A mountain pink
 crawls out of green stone
  tottering.

And then, and then:
 a trembling woodfern
  a blue-spruce sapling,

the hint
 of
  rain.

~ Vince Clemente

Visiting With Walt

I

Walking through fields rich with clover
where cows grazed on sweet moist straw,
with child raw courage and chilled flesh,
I came to your door but did not knock.

Unguarded, laden with dried weeds
and debris gathered from walnut trees,
I entered your empty house and drew a fresh fire
in the chalk ash broken brick hearth.

Bursting flames and earth-odor smoke
filled the room, casting accordion shadows
caressing, filling, the void with solace.
Black shadows alive, dancing on aged walls.

I talked to you, crawling into your words,
and in my loneliness the flames whispered your poems.
Rising, breaking flames silently regained power,
and the fire licked the air, popping and hissing.

Your secrets escaped. I knew yours
and told you mine, and the smell of mildew fell
deafly into the clover from the flowering fields
where cows pastured and cast their eyes knowingly.

II

A half century has passed and I visit your house again.
The fields of clover, the walnut trees now gone.
I find myself in the fireplace room
where you burned thoughts and poems -

The walls are painted white, covering old scars.
I remember the fireflames ... the long black shadows.
The shadows now play grey against white walls.

Working with words, my anguish matches yours ---
The fire hisses ... weary, igniting combusted gases.

The smell of clover and smoke of walnut warms,
and your words live on, carefully placed,
on pads of dreams and dignified disguise.

In a room lined with seeking worshippers,
who stand in front of the closed fireplace,
I hear their stories, but listen, listen
for echoes of so long ago.

~ Jeanette Klimszewski

A Walk in the River

*I think heroic deeds were all conceiv'd in the open air,
and all free poems also...*
>   from "Song of the Open Road"

Great deeds invoked like poetry in the open air,
arise like mighty rays to span the arc of stars across the holding skies

One small being fixed on this earth, a walk in the river, and one great
    deed radiating out and out and out
while life streams seamlessly through blinking eyes-
    a sensual, filmless feed.

The movie folding back on itself, one screen out there
    the other lit within,
riding out this stereo admixture to the end
you daydream through the lifestream bouncing fantasy off of sensation
    to a soundtrack of unexpected musics:
a branch's sigh, sprinkled laughter, clips of talk, cars through the rain,
    streetlamps humbuzzing you along
applause, footsteps
doors open, doors close
a phone rings and rings... you answer
no one's there.

Before you now a sparkling basket
    hinting at a secret inside, a silence waiting to be wooed
like a cobra creepy and hooded,
the silence coils, charmed and swaying it takes you in
    as the thoughtstream rides out into the sea
    and the lifestream finds its cadence

simple Silence bearing witness to the Great River
    surged by the Two Streams.

One small being
A walk in the river
A great deed.

Radiating out and out and out
Like rays of light
Spanning the arc of stars across the holding skies.

~ Andrea Rowen

On a Rainy Day, If Whitman Went to the Mall

O, Whitman, you'd love the holes in the $100 dollars jeans they sell,
you could rub your own knee or have thousands of lovers rub it for you,
never mind that they tore it and charged you double, in America
    we are free to rub our knees!
O, Whitman, with a cell-phone you could call comrades in Malaysia,
    Australia, comrades in Russia, oh my god, it's Russia now!
Or maybe it was then too, what do i know, hardly anyone knows
    geography in America!
Anywhere, you can call anywhere! You can buy a big round cookie for
    like two dollars, or a computer, where *Leaves of Grass* as an e-book
    could be called *Fiber-Optics of Megabytes*.

O, Whitman, in the corner of a bookstore of your marble mall your
    Leaves of Grass still shines,
and in the parking lot there is a patch of grass that shines, and there
    really are still leaves of grass if you look for them,
if you will take off your boots and walk barefoot
    there is grass, still plenty of grass, O, Whitman!

    ~ Mankh

Searching for Absolutes

Buying steak
I tease the meaty textures
on the plastic wrap,
admiring the droplets behind
their drip-proof seal.
Lugging my life through
self-service aisles, I
see Walt and Allen, both,
among the bargains: Marrow
and meal, greens and glassware,
coffee spoons unmetaphoric,
5 off the price as market-
euphoric. Intensity among
the canned goods and sweetly
scented sprays.

I wait with cart amid
the patient hordes
to make my declaration.
The freckle-faced girl,
her fingers bouncing over
my private things, pushes
me into double bags. Keeper
of the gate, she calls me to account.

~ David B. Axelrod

Looking for Walt Whitman at C.W. Post

If you want me again look
for me under your boot-soles.
                from "Song of Myself"

I went looking for you, Walt,
all over campus after we read
your Paumanok poems.

Not far from where I once sat
at the top of a stone stair reciting
"Give Me the Splendid Silent Sun,"
I saw boot prints in the mulch
of flower beds in the formal garden
beside the administration building.

In the woods along
the arboretum walk, I picked up
those tracks again and swear
I could hear your bardic voice
trill and catalogue the names
of American hardwoods
as if you were reciting
the names of the saints.

In the recesses of the library
stacks I spied your gray-bearded
presence peering into volumes
of experimental poems from
the heart of the continent.

Walking down the hall
where one class door was ajar
I saw a familiar colleague
with his mouth wide open
but heard you declaring
to his wide-eyed students
our independence from
Old World hegemony

and insisting we must open
our doors more to immigrants
and those the system despises
and let our instincts speak
more fully without check.

I was afraid, Walt, what kind
of revolution you might foment.

I opened my mouth to issue
a warning to the young about
the potential danger of your
influence, but all that came out
were words I recognized as yours,

I bequeath myself to the dirt
to grow from the grass I love,

and I knew that wherever I stepped
on this campus and your Island
I would always be touching you.

~ Norbert Krapf

Whitman's Photograph Speaks

All the way down Atlantic Avenue I pressed the record key
until the turn at Flatbush, made my way up
the parking ramps, reeking of the poor living in its wells.

I was one of the endless stream of commuters driving
Brooklyn's streets, while the morning sun cut through
the clotted air, a ghetto of open lesions, bandaged
with sunlight, a grief I escaped each evening, like a bat
from a burial cave.

Families living in cardboard boxes. Blood stains on corners.
I locked the car doors before the traffic lights;
the homeless waited to clean windshields with their spit,
a dollar the price to pass.

There were men in wheelchairs rolling down Atlantic Avenue,
calloused palms begging at car windows, street oil
anointing their hands.

Just like you, I recorded what I saw, backdrops of a city
with broken windows. So many windows, they covered them
with fake fresco paintings of flowerpots, cats sitting on the sills.

This, our America, passing its cup at streetlights,
begging at car windows, soiled rags and spit to clean
windshields, the shattered sleeping beneath The New York Times.

I grasped death on those mornings allowing it to enter;
took the gauze from my tongue, felt the rawness of my teeth
as I tried to speak but was already in the grave and the voice
speaking was yours.

From the photograph above my desk you looked at me.
I heard you call my name and stumbled out to meet you,
rattling death from my body.

~ Gladys Henderson

The Voice in Wind and Waves

Sargassum floats in rhythm
Of waves, tangled between my toes
With strands of algae, as I watch
The tide ebb of his beloved life.

Inland, I follow in the pilgrimage
Of this timeless traveler and celebrate
The face of poetry, transformed
In the deep gaze beneath a bushy brow.

The Father of free verse,
Whose life was one long revision,
Using word-pause to escape
A backspace, returning in repetition,

Spontaneous as the breeze whistling
Through white oak trees.
And its Leaves blanket his homeground.
And gathered, they become his being.

I emerge in harmony with the cosmos,
Singing Songs of myself, hopeful to produce
Cloudbursts of joyous raindrops
To cultivate my bearded landscape.

And to my children, I will America.
And for their children, I place a brick
In his backyard, for each one,
To be the foundation of enlightenment.

But Walt, will they come?
Will they come, as I did?

~ Robert Savino

Into the Light: Safe Haven 1944

And you that shall cross from shore to shore
years hence are more to me,
and more in my meditations, than you might suppose.
~ Walt Whitman

Thank God for you, *Henry Gibbins*,
your decks laden with my bedraggled brethren dark and fair,
tall and short, frail-boned and lean -- each and every one of us
reborn in the wake of conscience.
Blessed, your ship of dreams bedecked
with these 982 holocaust survivors and their leader, Ruth Gruber.
Praised -- her leader, Franklin Delano Roosevelt
and you, Captain Korn, your kind face and outstretched arms;
your smiling crew -- their helpful hands;
your great vessel -- its lustrous wood halls and stalwart bulk,
sky-crowned decks surrounded by sea-speckled rail
a far cry from barbed wire.
Divine are you -- clean fresh air that fills sunken chests
and lungs ashen from the fires of Auschwitz-Birkenau,
Bergen-Belsen, Buchenwald, Dachau, Treblinka...
the stain never to wash out.
And you, glistening-white toilets -- a sight for the sore eyes
of those who've known the cast-iron pots
of the iron-rimmed camps, the stench of memory.
You -- buoyant sea, revered for strong currents and changing tides,
your gulls that glide the breeze and assuage wounded spirit.
"Are you America?" asks each wary sojourner;
and you, dining halls bejeweled with vegetables,
cornucopia of meats, kaleidoscope of sweets
that swell shrunken bellies, smooth withered souls
"Are you America too?"

Soft pillows and ample blankets nestled deep in hammocks,
the nightmares you help smother,
sweet dreams you set in motion
"Are you?"
Oh, most wondrous throng -- your huddled masses -- my ancestry,
it is *you* who are America! My America!

~ Ruth Sabath Rosenthal

poet's note:
The Henry Gibbins was a ship within a naval convoy that carried 982 of the neediest holocaust refugees out of Europe into the US and to the Island of Manhattan in August 1944, at which point, they were transported by train to Oswego, NY and there spent over a year in Ft. Ontario, refugee camp. The exodus, named "Safe Haven," was authorized by Congress at the request of President Franklin Delano Roosevelt and organized by a woman named Ruth Gruber, whom he'd appointed. These "token" survivors of the holocaust were all the US was allowed to take in, and not permanently at that; however, upon Roosevelt's death, President Truman persuaded Congress to legislate that any of the 982 could remain in the US and apply for citizenship.

Poets Gone

I

Where have they gone the poets who
stumbled to readings drunk as hatters yet
recited flawlessly with dignity and clarity
(they are in schools teaching adolescents)

where is the poet who monkeyed up
the fire escape, leapt in the window
and stole away the doctor's wife
(he is negotiating a deal for a third family car)

where is the poet who owned no shoes in winter
but an overcoat in summer, had no place to sleep
or need to sleep, whose words raised bumps on the skin
(he is mailing the mortgage check)

where is the poet who burned as the sun
while he read in the hall, eager and ready
to service some ladies after the reading
(he trudges the Mall with an ample wife)

where is Mackie who died in a Village bar quarreling
over a sonnet, Sally who died of exposure and cold
after the Professor tossed her from the dinner party,
the Boston Fox who died of too much good heroin,

Jack who lived on the subway and sold poems in saloons,
Banyon who walked out a window chasing a psychedelic mirage,
where are they now, where are their poems,
(gone and forgotten, the poems dust).

II

The field is full of polygoose,
the night is filled with stars.
It's said the ghost of Yeats is loose
in small town Irish bars.

It's said the shade of Auden roams
around Smithhaven Mall,
haunting poets who've quit their jobs
to walk before they crawl.

It's said the wraith of Whitman rides
the D train night and day
running fingers through his beard.
His ancient eyes are gay.

It's said old Ezra's spirit tall
and spare has found true rest,
boots up beneath hard earth
he lies, head East, feet West.

The day is filled with points of light
the lawn is home to doves
who strut and preen and clear their throats
to sing, and sing of love.

~ Ray Freed

Walt Whitman Among the Reaching Hands

Walt is between the army cots in the field tent.
The soldiers are passing from one life to another.
The tent fills with sawing to the bone.
He holds a bloody bandage and kisses it tenderly.
He opens the tent flaps like morning fog.
He sits on an amputated tree stump.
A drummer boy watches Walt make a piece of grass whistle.
The boy points to the battle, "What can you do about that?"
He straps a drum as he races to the front lines.

There is nothing he can do about it.
The morning is cold as bullets.
He hears the drumming of a woodpecker on dead trees.
There is nothing to do about the cut timber and bone.

He wants to return to the outstretched hands.
He notices the dead field mouse curled into a comma.
What could he do about that?
The crosses are a line of type he could set piece by piece
until they were pebbles in clear water.
He had felt a man break at sunrise and now his hands
were useless to do much about what was happening.

Walt removed his leather boots and thick woolen socks,
plunged his feet into mud to take root as blackberries.
This is what he could do about it!
For a moment, all is still.
It is the kind of quiet that makes a deer notice.
Even the boy dying on the red blanket of grass notices.

~ Martin Willitts, Jr.

O how shall I warble myself for the dead one I loved?

> ~ Walt Whitman
> from "When Lilacs Last in the Dooryard Bloom'd"

America's carol of mourning,
Thrush's flute song
from pond in Long Island Pine Barrens,
from alcove of pine and white cedar

I walk the Barrens Whitman knew,
think of framed photograph on my living room mantle,
my mother, her brown hair
bobbed over her forehead, she looks down
on child in her lap,
her softness pressed against my back

Thirty-two years she had

I hike to pond
banked with high bush blueberry,
listen for poet,
for singer

In this cloister
the Hermit's "long, loud, liquid-clear" prelude,
then high splintering as if pieces from ecclesiastical glass

~ Maxwell Corydon Wheat, Jr.

poet's note:
I heard the Hermit Thrush sing from bushes by a pond in the Long Island Pine Barrens on a spring night when Venus was showing over the western horizon as Walt Whitman saw the planet over our Nation's Capital that April of Abraham Lincoln's assassination. Writing a feature story about this for *Newsday* I asked Lorna Salzmann, environmentalist, and her husband, Eric Salzmann, musician, author of article, "Sweet Singer of the Pine Barrens," about the Hermit Thrush, *Terra Nova: Nature & Culture* - Summer 1997, if they could guide me to a pond where I could hear this song which F. Schuyler Matthews, in his book, <u>Field Book of Wild Birds and Their Music</u> (G. P. Putman's Sons, New York, N. Y., 1904, 1921), writes of "the wonderful way

the singer delivers his sustained tonic and then embroiders it with a rapid and brilliant cadenza." This is the song Whitman presents as the refrain, each time in different words, in his long and lovely poem mourning the death of Abraham Lincoln, "When Lilacs Last in the Dooryard Bloom'd."

Walt, you are my gestalt
    you are my salt
     you are my malt
your *Leaves of Grass*
are my universal pass.

~ Darrel Blaine Ford

Unfinished Story

It seems to me more than all the print I have read in my life.
  "Song of Myself" #13 ~ Walt Whitman

I read the sound of the sea
letters dancing on a pinhead.
Squint at green twigs
between white flowers
telling a bedtime story

the crunch of the acorn
broken by a squirrel in early morning,
the underside of a poem on my desk
by a poet who puts me to shame
with his phrases like melted butter.

I read the palm of an artist who has
tattoos on each finger
like the wristlet worn by a
soldier going into battle who lives
close by minus a century or two

the throat and breast of robins
who typewrite on the lawn in script
older than all the birds and me
who live next to the pumping well
in lonely farmhouse yard.

I read the beard of a poet on the cover
of *Poets & Writers* and think the answer
can be found in his curly white hair or
on the closed window keeping out a dirty
spring day filled with pollen

the house with the giant tree,
covering the yard of the hidden old man
who I erase and whatever message
he is sending wrapped in sticky
sap wrappers from the rankly trunk.

I read the Braille story written on the
neighbor's fence and although she's nice
she may die before me and what will
become of the conversations
leading to the final page?

~ Evelyn Kandel

A Love Song for Walt Whitman's Mother

My mother look'd in delight and amazement at the stranger...
The more she look'd upon her she loved her...
Never before had she seen such wonderful beauty and purity...
But the red squaw never came nor was heard of there again.
                        ~ Walt Whitman, from "The Sleepers"

You who sat by the window and waited, hours you waited,
    days and weeks and months you waited.
Sometimes you idled when you should have been sewing or sweeping,
    thought of the amber morning she came to your doorstep,
    tall and strong-limbed, eyes like candlewicks,
    light flashing from the tips of black,
    the tone of her voice, exotic as Egyptian lotuses,
    a bundle of rushes carried on her back
    like the stiff wheat of a grain-goddess.

She wanted to work— offered to rush-bottom chairs,
    you asked her to sit on the fireside bench, lean and loafe awhile
    talk together in syllables falling like half-notes onto the floor.
Even years of sweeping could not rid those buckling fibers of the talk.
You wanted her for your friend, another young woman like yourself—
    but so unlike in the best of ways—
    would have given anything to have her to sing or laugh with
    as you worked each of your young days closer to age, grave.
You cooked for her— made the best meal you could, however meager,
    gave her no work to do, only fondness to take away
    as she left sometime around three and never returned,
    you watched her western path even after she faded from view.

Sometimes, you imagined the sunset was secretly holding
    the earth tones of her rosy skin
    or that the ink-spills of night were keeping her,
    blending the richness of her hair with the charcoal of darkness.

You made lists of explanations for why she never returned,
    counted the reasons and stars like wampum in the sky,
    a covenant belt, a promise, purple and white
    sky and planets woven like seashells on buckskin.

She would have returned if she could, Louisa.
She would have made you a belt to wear around your hips—
    wampum women holding hands, side by side, joined in amity,
    stitched, woven,
    fastened around your waist, a sturdy flower-chain.
You would have fashioned her a friendship quilt
    with binding, without bias,
    appliquéd with a pattern of stars
    with your name, Louisa, embroidered in the center.
It would have warmed her on cold winter nights.
She would have returned if she could have, Louisa.
You know well the many things that might have kept her away.
Fear, sickness, marriage, child-rearing, work, even, say it— death,
    or, worst of all,
    the lack of desire to return.

But it wasn't the last, Louisa. You, daughter of Dutch farmers, and she,
    the Native American beauty
    would be joined
    to that morning when you sat together
    bound in a covenant chain
    made from the milky white of whelks
    and violet of quahog,
    bound in a quilt
    made from scraps of cloth
    and bright folds of fabric—
    neither gift given, both gifts received.

    ~ Annabelle Moseley

Have the past struggles succeeded?
What has succeeded? yourself? your nation? Nature?

~ Walt Whitman, from "Song of the Open Road"

Walking My Open Road

Have the past struggles succeeded?
I dare say they have not;
they have, however, bowed my once unbendable back.

When dreams turned into nightmares,
with no mother to wake and comfort me
Nature rocked me in her arms
gave me a safe place to sleep.

When set upon by my father, as by a thief,
no righteous man was there to hear my wails.
Nature brought me through the torrents of pain
sheltered me within the woods
where he would not step foot
fearing the creatures that lived within.

When I walked the path of self-destruction,
using any vice I could
I would be stopped short by Nature whispering
that there were more reasons to live than reasons to die
so I slowly pulled back from the abyss that six of my siblings
could not find the footing to do so.

And when woman and man's machine ran down my oldest child
I tried with all my might to leave this plane of existence,
only to be brought back with man's ingenious machines that pump
life back into lifeless frames of grieving mothers' bodies,
to be blinded by the white light in the white room was all too much.

From that day of my "rebirth" to this, I have decided that Nature
is not done with me, sharing her secrets and her plans.
I must walk out the rest of the years till my natural conclusion,
and I will do so with a joyous heart and a poem in my pocket
and some time to spare to stop by the woods
that have always been my home and rest a spell.

  ~ Tammy Nuzzo-Morgan
    7/2/06

"fish-shape Paumanok"

i had fish for dinner
we ate by the ocean
there were fish everywhere
i celebrate that and the waiter and the water.

~ Mankh

The Walt Whitman Birthplace

In the off hours,
the local cats
would scourge
the terrain,
flip over
themselves for
fireflies in twilight.
The nights
rang twice:
once for us,
caretakers and
caregivers,
and once for
him, a boy
in cloth diapers first
and later
inquisitive
and bold,
full of long
lines and
dirty beards.
And when
the doorbell rang,
we knew
the possibility
of it was low,
but we were
high, high, high
for what might be
on the other side.

~ Alan Semerdjian

poet's note:
Alan spent some time as caretaker of The Walt Whitman Birthplace State Historic Site and Interpretive Center - three years worth of taking out the garbage in the evenings, curating experimental art shows, and chasing ghosts.

Walt Whitman's Daughters

On an eleventh-month afternoon
on Paumanok we trade impressions
of Walt nurturing a runaway slave
and juxtaposing that episode
with the incident of a well-to-do
woman hiding behind the curtains
of her fine house while in her fantasies
she gives herself to twenty-eight
young men splashing in the salt
water not far beyond her window

and I look up from my text
and see across the desk from me
two young women, one Puerto Rican,
one Navajo, their dark eyes ablaze,
one pair round as full moons,
the other parallel ripe almonds,
huddling together close as sisters
brought together by kindred spirits
and the distance from their homes

and I understand better than ever
before how a kelson of the creation
is indeed love and that all men
and women are brothers and sisters
and that a man is rich in proportion
to the number of daughters and sons
he can admit into his affection and
carry with him as he journeys forth
every day the rest of his life

and I, a native Midwesterner,
conclude that a country
that can produce a poet like
Walt Whitman from an Island
off the East Coast who brings us
together to share our perceptions

from different perspectives
and bloodlines and places
so far apart in so many ways
is richer than I ever imagined.

~ Norbert Krapf

Father of Us All

You were the first
to not, like Emerson, have
one foot in the old world.

You hyped your wares without shame
even as your books languished
in a corner on the printer's floor.

You capitalized on the slenderest of threads
to see yourself transformed
from teacher, nurse, newspaperman
--to "good gray poet."

Such embracing vision
and an eye for the tiniest of details!

Never married, never sire of a child,
you came and still come to us wearing wings
and we have followed you.

More than avuncular, more than paternal,
more than muse, Walt, you are my father,
father of us all.

~ Charlene Babb Knadle

Beyond the palisade

steep in a cup of fragrant leaves, meld the brown gold riches,
steep in the depths of Paumanok's wood
follow the path to Jayne's Hill, breathe the musty loam of leaves
in underbrush, sated, return to these walls,
shelter within the palisade that protects
from urban sprawl, from unruly crowds that
follow your path from sea to sound
steep in the cup of warm wood, smoothed brick, split shingles

words pour like chamomile into old china,
words like leaves spiral in windblown eddies,
reel on clipped lawn, flow in tidal surge from hand to pale papyrus --
words like lovers, embrace in passion's song

beyond the palisade,
the hills, the brooks, wood and valley, ocean and bay
within these walls time slows,
within this vessel take rest,
renewed, fly past the palisade, run through the fields,
cross the roads and streams,
walk the way of Whitman

~ Ann Kenna

editor's note
Jayne's Hill, the highest point on Long Island, is located in West Hills, about a mile due west of Whitman's birthplace. Whitman mentions walking there in *Specimen Days*. Today part of a county park and a wooded promontory along a ridge of high hills, in Whitman's day it was possible to see the Long Island Sound to the north, and the Atlantic Ocean to the south, from its height.

Writing Helps

We came from the city as the potato farms receded
Open fields gave way to a construction site
My time of play in the dirt mounds
Holes became big puddles that froze for ice skating
A landscape changing, soon filled with steel girders,
A framework for a shopping center that would bear your name
While across the highway, your childhood home
remained fixed in time
A main room that doubled for cooking and relaxing
The short beds upstairs I wanted to touch
The precious books on desks and tables
Did your mother and father read to you there by the firelight?
Did you play in the grass outside?
I tramped through the woods of West Hills near your home,
pretending that I, too, had a beard and big hat

In seventh grade I imitated some of your language for an essay I wrote,
What the Flag Means to Me --
A partial line still comes to mind --
"It means the soldiers, the sailors, the stewards..."
and I officially began my own writing journey

It was in elementary school that I'd first read your words,
then studied them more closely in high school
A college friend gave me a copy of *Leaves of Grass* – I still have it
Years later I visited your final home on Mickle Street in Camden,
    New Jersey
I remember a hat resting on a straight-backed wooden chair
In those last years you were photographed with long white hair and
    flowing beard,
your poetic reputation assured, only to grow much larger in the
    20th Century

I long for the peace of the grass in your front yard on Long Island
I try to find it as an adult and not just in childhood memories
How can the boy stay in the man without getting stuck in nostalgia?
How can nature soothe amidst the noise of my own clutter,
and the chaos of the city?
Writing helps
Thank you

~ Mark Donnelly

Ode to a Dandelion

I believe a leaf of grass is no less than the journeywork of the stars...
                                              ~ Walt Whitman

The ordinary dandelion
a weed throughout the world
plucked with annoyance, even distemper
by landscapers, lovers of perfection.

Rising on milky hollow stems,
golden flowers brighten the day
and when they dry --
a second life,
a white puffball forms.

Soft globular dome reminiscent of mounds,
mounds that hold back the ocean's summer tide
to protect a child's sandcastle from crumbling,
mounds whose circumference
is the minute reincarnation of mountains.

Mounds of radiance, its head a globe of white light
light trapped between hair like threads
light filling the fluffy ends, each one in perfect symmetry
each a broomy flowerette forming a circle of breath
---yet steadfast & with such force the silken stems remain intact
---when blown upon their fluffy ends ruffle and ribbon.

When turned over, their silken struts
defy the network of steel cables crisscrossing
to build a framework for bridges.
These silk strands the journeywork of stars, of God,
of evolution in its most clever phase.

This flower, this weed, this marvel of beauty,
starts a wondering about reincarnation --
migration from yellow blossom to white fluffy dome.
When enough days have passed
and winds wahool, the broomy stuff will sail off
leaving silken stems, like ribs on toy paper umbrellas,
gone their canopy, gone the flowerettes
floating on air's currents, like floating fairies
like magical totems too light to be caught
too airy to be held, too beautiful to last
but oh, how it engraves itself in the heart.

~ Muriel Harris Weinstein

Stranded at the Walt Whitman Mall

I was distracted, passed my station
got off the train
at an unfamiliar destination
caught a bus back
to an approximate location
that much closer to my intended goal.

I was shivering, tired, hungry, perplexed;
directly in front of me
my eye caught some text:

O cruel . . . O helpless soul of me! . . .

What perfection! What harmony —
a poet's words carved in stone, blazoned
on the wall outside the Walt Whitman mall.

Rise up fellow poets! Write poems
along paths, at bus stops, in junkyards
on stones and bleached bones — show up
in store windows, outside barbershop doors —
cavalcade through the streets of our towns.

~ Barbara Southard

Autumn (just about a mile from the Mall)

Walt Whitman is outside on his lawn
wool sweater on, rake in hand
watching a car drive away -
he could have chosen to go along but
on such a crisp autumn day
it was more than he could stand

for the eponymous mall would take its toll
with weekend sales and food-court crowds
distractions hungry enough to swallow
the universal soul

besides, Sunday chores and leaves abound
leaves on lawns, in gutters, leaves cover flowerbeds
wet leaves fill cellar stairwells, leaves hide stone paths that
lead nowhere except to the source of more leaves
bright as fire

he moves lightly
with Tai Chi steps
a sneaker dance with shoulder jerks
the bamboo tines catch and flex
drag brittle flames, rust red waves
manhandled into piles waist-high to be
ignominiously bagged

Walt Whitman is outside on his lawn
wool sweater on, rake in hand
watching a car drive away -
he could have chosen to go along but
on such a crisp autumn day
it was more than he could stand

for susurrus winds send spiraling leaves to earth
a quiet pond smiles to the sky
in obscurity, dark swans in song rehearse

~ Anthony Policano

Walt and the Wheelbarrow of Poetry

The wheelbarrow wheels clack on cobblestones,
sounding like the wheel of the hand letterpress
as it presses the lips of the type across the bow of blank paper
until it leaves an indelible song so hidden,
only the ear-trumpet of the daffodils can hear it for what it is.

This is the same message a lover brings to me, shimmering, the same words
still moist from his lips, dipping into me with the thrust
of a hummingbird's beak. Oh, my lover brings me such intense joy,
the sun blushes the color of cobblestones. His secret is the comfort of lovers
enfolding into each other until they merge as one.

It is like dipping for a long bath, these words impressed into pages
so deep you can feel the memory of the type. If you listen
you could hear the faint hum of hummingbird wings glistening with dew.
This message can be raised as a font,

or nude as a blank paper, or singing a poem under your breath,
until it brings goosebumps as I am wrapped in my lovers arms.
I am embarrassed at my display of emotions.
However my lover greets me as if bored with my excitement.

My heart comes to a sudden halt, like type kissing paper
realizing it is over, like a song reaching a crescendo and it is
the same disappointment I feel while wheeling
a barrow filled with its lung full of my poetry
hoping someone will notice and listen to its song.

The same disenchantment when people ignore it
like a lover rejecting my greetings. It is the same rejection
all lovers fear and expect, and hope never happens.
Rather I never write another line than face this refusal
both personal and impersonal as a lover's last kiss.

People cannot understand my urge to speak of lovers,
how a person can both be male and female,
how words can clack on cobblestones. It is
the rise and fall of a heaving chest after love is exhausted,
fingers tingling like individual picas of type.

It is then when you notice that spokes always gravitate to a center,
that the axle spins as a sun like the iris of the eye,
that it is not the hummingbird hanging in mid-air
but rather the air holding its breath as if stunned by rejection.

I could walk barefoot across the coarseness of small uneven pebbles
and never feel them.
I could be amazed by how a speck of sand in the corner of my eye
could make it twitch as a grasshopper. But my lover turning away
is something I can never fully understand.

~ Martin Willitts, Jr.

Flying Island

Washington lost his first battle near Jamaica, Queens.

Colonials pushed 'cross & up Manhattan to Fort Washington
over to Fort Lee, Jersey & down, boating the Delaware to PA.

They were "times that tried men's souls."

The War turned at Trenton.

Flash foward: Lindbergh left Roosevelt Field for Paris.

Howard Hughes, Jimmy Doolittle and Amelia Earhart
schmoozed in, out and around Island airports while

Grumman in Bethpage, Republic in Farmingdale plus Island
others went west and east to help win the war.

Einstein, a neighbor, helping cross the Hudson at Princeton.

Apollo's LM left Bethpage for six moon landings.

Macadam of Roosevelt Field covering footsteps,

tire tracks & wings of courageous and anxious souls

while ignorant buyers, buy, buy unaware of sacred ground.

Walt Whitman turns over in his grave; see HIS 110 mall?

Ask the Canarsie, the Shinnecock or the Poospatuck Indian.

They were here, before we went asphalt and concrete crazy.

One long runway from Brooklyn to Montauk Point.

~ Richard Savadsky

End of Day

Many hours pass from dawn breaking the spell of night,
many moments move to shade under oak limbs when the sun is high,
many images crowd my mind as dusk knocks on the open barn doors,
night mist surrounds me, I have done all I can this day,
plowed a field with sweat slick upon my brow,
picked apples from the orchard alive with sweet blossoms,
tended livestock with water, feed, and a few good words,
a wagon wheel mended, harness straps rebraided;
I have heard the warble of birdsong,
smelled the perfume of lilacs blooming,
sat upon a field of grass, watched brown ants summit blades of green,
thrown my head back in praise of air, love, and nature;
sang a song of myself for the heavens to echo,
crickets accompany me, a spotted hawk swoops by;
I am alive in this moment of passing,
"splendor of ended day floating and filling me,"
a "Song at Sunset."

~ J R Turek

Walt Whitman:
"Of Life immense in passion, pulse, and power..."

from Inscriptions, "One's-Self I Sing"

Celebrating the earth, he is all of us and ours throughout all time.
The land and the sky and sea and mountain,
grass's greenness, leaves' brown. The carpenter, the lawyer,
boatswain, fiddler and the cattle rancher, too.

He is today's breath. Tomorrow's fanciful thought.
He is the soul nurturer and that soul's body, too.
He is America's tribute and the words that sing those praises.
Its raw consciousness and lost conscience. Its muscle and misery.

He is its heart beating softly and its screaming soaring need.
The rich black soil that buries our feet
and the cool mist raining down moisture on our lips.
He is our Spring's warmth and Winter blight,
the ripe fruit of Summer and over-ripe bounty of Fall.

His is the stifling heat of midday; the felt dampness of dusk.
The spent laborer and the fresh born child.
The tireless physician and the gambler's greed.
Tolling man's virtue and embracing his vice,
it's all as one to the democracy of his pen.

The chronicler of the live oak and the whisper of the dead sea,
he also chants of the bear and the bird and the buffalo.
He is forest's cool dawn awakening,
and evening's sun-warmed drowsiness.
The feeding infant and his mother's warm breast.
The lover's yearning and the sate of that desire.

He sounds the beat of horse hooves and the whirr of wind-sails.
Walks the narrowness of city streets and its broadest thoroughfares.
He is faithful advocate, singing of vistas, new and near,
and those far off from view.

His are the eyes that see and that which is seen.
The ears that hear and that which is heard.
The mind that knows and the mouth that speaks
 of the tenderness of touch.
Alchemist of time, he is the voice down the ages.

Bard of the sierras and savannahs, the prairies and the plains,
big cities and small towns are his purview.
Friend of brothers and sisters everywhere, he is companion
 to all equally.
He cries of war and warriors, those voices silenced, and those in pain.
Peace-givers are extolled, but so are the merciless and unforgiven.

He strolls the beaches of Long Island, Brooklyn's heights, and beyond.
Climbs the grand mountains of the west and sails forth from the vast
 coastal sea.
Suffers the sweat of southern plantations and the frostbite
 of northern woods.
Muse of poets everywhere, he speaks only for himself, but not
 of himself alone.

His is the vision through which we wander, wonder and see,
and seize upon like sky. He abides and abandons, too.
Being here and then not, he has become us . . . Forever and for all.
His own rich legacy, and ours, he is the poet's immortality.

~ Genevieve Shore

Watching the Stars Go By

*speeding through space, speeding
through heaven and the stars*
~ Whitman

webbed with silver rays
noble walled plains
and craters
the moon's loneliness
more desolate than the Sahara
hangs in blackness

I walk the Milky Way
speeding through space
speeding through heaven
picking up stars
and lost souls
searching for a way
back to Earth

Looking for a spark
in your eyes
to tell me you are
here for me too
when I am lost
watching the stars

~ Rita Katz

Walt Whitman Was a River (#489)

Walt Whitman was a river
Ferocious and boisterous - tenacious
Unyielding, unbending
"Out of the Cradle, Endlessly Rocking . . .
Are you whispering it, and have been all the time, you sea-waves?
Is that it from your liquid rims and wet sands?"
Yet, bent
And bent down
Down, down,
Ever deeper down
Ever excoriating the depths of Earth
Deepening Nature
Walt Nature
Nature to write
Written into the ground
Deeper
Inside the soft ground
Until he is the Basalt
    - the Smithtown Clay -
Beneath it all.
Cutting, forming - beginning
Absorbing the Earth
Becoming it
Becoming all of which we know
"I effuse my flesh in eddies, and drift in lacy jags . . .
Failing to fetch me at first, keep encouraged,
Missing me one place, search another,
I stop somewhere, waiting for you."
Coring out the old
Nestling
Becoming comfortable
Comfortably new

And people reigned
And people rained
On him
Gather people
Gather around him
Gather around the puddle

Now forming, foaming
New formed puddle
Walt, mucking about in the mud
Lashing, licking up at the rindle
Water, life-blood, huddled
Accumulating girth
Of reflection
People looking down on him
And in
Seeing themselves
What they are
Walt, they are
In the rivulet
Mustering strength, sincerity
Superfluity of ebb and flow
Increasing intensity
Brook-born
Population taking notice
Of course, intent
No longer drifting
But freshet quickwater
Congregating delegation of critics
And recruiters
Decide Walt is big enough
Drilling him
Peers now appear
For the footbridge to cross over
Streaming, current
The deluge breaks free
But with Ginsberg's reference
"Ah, dear father, graybeard, lonely old courage-teacher,
what America did you have when Charon quit poling his ferry and
you got out on a smoking bank and stood watching the boat
disappear on the black waters of Lethe?"

This river runs rampant
And free
Inside the cavernous gorge created
Inside the canyon of knowledge
Lonely abyss

Aching, aching for home
Reeling on the thought
That someday, we will understand
We will build on the sand
Rise above the tide
Taking strides
Taking perception
"I perceive I have not really understood any thing, not a single object, and that no man ever can,
Nature here in sight of the sea taking advantage of me to dart . . ."
Darting truth home
Through ocean foam
Is where we find ourselves,
You, Walt, and us.

~ Douglas G. Swezey

Sing to my soul, renew its languishing faith and hope,
Rouse up my slow belief, give me some vision of the future,
Give me for once its prophecy and joy . . .

Hymns to the universal god from universal man—all joy!
A reborn race appears—a perfect, world, all joy!
Women and men in wisdom innocence and health—all joy!

~ Walt Whitman, "The Mystic Trumpeter"- Stanza 8

New Hymns for the Promised Land

Come to this place to vent deleted passion
Bring a wallet of justice to barter down the hardwood from the cruel
Here no torment goes unrecorded, no betrayal unknown
And a good listener drinks wisdom like gin waiting for the news.

So leave your ashen trousers on the wormwood floors
Leave your tight raised fist and the echoing mines behind
Leave off where you started, there's something old calling
A radiance, a name, a diamond coal train
Full throttle charge through the meadow by day.

On the stove two more agreements are simmering
While night smokes restless under half drawn shades
A crazy bird sounds against the tin darkness
And lamp light glares cold off the window panes.

We ponder, lick our lips with wonder
Time scribbles across our brows
And we watch the distance between us grow younger
As sunrise washes clouds ginger and we finger the clouds.

I'm going between us again, I'm checking the miles
I'm going between us again, to see if God is still there
I'm going between us again, wishing you here,
posting messages in midair.

A waitful gladness still here.
(a pressing heart regarding blue circles in the sand)
A grateful madness still here.
(a pilgrim angel singing new hymns for the promised land)

~ Andrea Rowen

Song for Walt Whitman

i imagine an empty stream of twilight spills mercy into the harbor of your lost children just in time to watch the half-light of morning explode into american suns and harborflowers the hull of sky above your head crashing white as waves or an unrealistic corona from punquogue to ellis island to camden all the forgotten stars twinkling capably forgotten stars and gaslamps and expectations fueled with laws and blue ambition tiffany glass streetlights traffic signals! you came to me with your arms half-open walked out of a splintered clamshell of dreams bearing a formula for the future world never wondering what had to be discarded the green song of a previous century the last good war ended centuries ago ever since the nation has suffered infestations manifestations and incantations while the planet reeled drunk with its progress through heaven you have slept unconcernedly in a seedless noon violated in the usual unswept hallway while men with money scoured the land stripsearched the soil ransacked the farms in a birth forest the rattling of great snakes the grinning irrelevent movement of ferrets while you walked casually with a sweet lumbering bear on the edge of a slumbering cliffside while you stood by a chokecherry tree superimposed with unstoppable youth and ambition like you i lit on the thumbs of the powerful a naked white butterfly juggling my wings like you an angel among dark birds incredible how simple to perch perfect straight and proud like you a ray of the one true sun surged through springwater with the power of being upwelling i saw you standing by the morning harbor a rising mist the song of buoys your song the antique creak of rudders your wooden oars singing i saw you in the immense morning the satisfaction of you stirred out of your honest sleep i saw you raise the jewel box of my expectations like a goblet toward an unrepentant heaven your heavy arms swung like a boom of peace no direction endless flow of lazy weather i was never a sailor but in that moment measuring the blue backwater of your imperfect wishes the sun was a fickle preoccupied god ignoring the momentary melodrama of the present time preposterous lover!
idiot nation! your shadow lingered on the poisoned embankment of my days your beach roses blossomed in the throes of my rebirth your sea your urchins your waving red ribbons! ah, the peninsular cries! ah, the human tide! we walked the beach once again together! we found love among intense empty beercans and the sad fish hooks of capitalism sweet grace of you, you, yes you! grace forced me skull and breath and shoulder to love you deeply grace and the pressure of your adoration

headfirst two palms thrust into rough pebbled sand the urgent salt
perfume of the wind after your skin tasting of tar and innocence and
insanity the empty kisses of your fortunate sun walt whitman i bite
down into the fleshy palm of your hand

~ George Wallace

essays

I had my choice when I commenc'd. I bid neither for soft eulogies, big money returns, nor the approbation of existing schools and conventions.

~ Walt Whitman
from "A Backward Glance o'er Travel'd Roads"

"Paumanok, and My Life On It As Child and Young Man"
(excerpts from the above titled essay which appears in *Specimen Days*)

~ Walt Whitman

The shores of this [south] bay, winter and summer, and my doings there in early life, are woven all through L. of G. ...

The eastern end of Long Island, the Peconic bay region, I knew quite well too—sail'd more than once around Shelter island, and down to Montauk—spent many an hour on Turtle hill by the old light-house, on the extreme point, looking out over the ceaseless Atlantic. I used to like to go down there and fraternize with the blue-fishers, or the annual squads of sea-bass takers.

More in the middle of the island were the spreading Hempstead plains, then (1830 – '40) quite prairie-like, open, uninhabited... yet plenty of fair pasture for the cattle, mostly milch-cows, who fed there by hundreds, even thousands...

Here, and all along the island and its shores, I spent intervals many years, all seasons, sometimes riding, sometimes boating, but generally afoot, (I was always then a good walker,) absorbing fields, shores, marine incidents, characters, the bay-men, farmers, pilots—always had a plentiful acquaintance with the latter, and with fishermen—went every summer on sailing trips—always liked the bare sea-beach, south side, and have some of my happiest hours on it to this day.

As I write, the whole experience comes back to me after the lapse of forty and more years—the soothing rustle of the waves, and the saline smell—boyhood's times, the clam-digging, barefoot, and with trowsers roll'd up—hauling down the creek—the perfume of the sedge-meaows—the hay-boat, and the chowder and fishing excursions;—or, of later years, little voyages down and out New York bay, in the pilot boats. Those same later years, also, while living in Brooklyn, (1836-'50) I went regularly every week in the mild seasons down to Coney island, at that time a long, bare unfrequented shore, which I had all to myself, and where I loved, after bathing, to race up and down the hard sand, and declaim Homer or Shakespeare to the surf and sea-gulls by the hour...

Starting From Sewanacky

~ Mankh

Starting from fish-shape Paumanok where I was born . . .
~ Walt Whitman

While Whitman helped to bring *Paumanok* -- one of the American Indian names for Long Island -- into the poetic mainstream consciousness, another name seems more appropriate: *Sewanacky*.

According to Evan T. Pritchard, in his wonderful book *Native New Yorkers*, "*Paumanok* is a term in the Renneiu language indicating "land of tribute," in reference to Long Island's role as a main source of the quohog and conch shells used in the manufacture of sewan or wampum, often used to pay tribute or taxes to another tribe. The people of Paumanok often had to pay tribute to the militarily superior people of the mainland." (Those superiors were probably the Mohawk and/or Iroquois.)

And, "*Paumanok* means the same thing as *Potomac* in the Powhatan language, "place where tribute is brought..." "

Since *Sewanacky* refers to the shell itself, and not the paying of tribute, this seems a more preferable name with which to honor some of the origins of Long Island and its peoples.

Considering that the shells were used for cultural and historical memory, covenant belts, badges of office and ceremonial devices, it seems obvious that the white wampum beads ("from the North Atlantic channeled whelk") and sewant beads ("black or dark purple") were also used to pay *real* tribute, as in respect and appreciation.

"The white shell beads of the whelk symbolized internal energies of peace, harmony, and contentment," and Sewant "symbolized the outside energies of a system" and "are made from the Poquahock, commonly known as the quahog, quahaug, or Western North Atlantic hard-shelled clam." (*Wikipedia* online).

Regardless of the meanings and usages, the land itself held (and still does) deep significance. Pritchard writes: "Paumanok, however, was clearly set apart from other areas of Turtle Island as especially sacred to the Algonquin from at least 1000 B.C.E., the dawning of Orient Point culture, onward."

The Shinnecock Indian Nation, "one of the oldest, continuously self-governing tribes in the country"(*shinnecocknation.com*), trace their ancestry back at least 10,000 years on Long Island.

According to Pritchard, "In ancient times, Long Island was called Matouac by some, Paumanok by others. Matouac means a "young man," or "the young warriors," referring to the younger tribes of the western half of the island."

And according to *longislandgenealogy.com*, another name for Long Island is said to be *Wamponomon*.

We can't blame Whitman, nor change his choice of nomenclature, but we can more closely touch the essence of the spirit of the daily lives and mystical connections of "The People" by remembering *Sewanacky*, as well as the others.

≈ ≈ ≈ ≈ ≈

Foreword to the *Countersong*

~ Jean Franco

The *Countersong to Walt Whitman* by the Dominican poet, Pedro Mir, was first published in Guatemala in 1952, not long before Colonel Castillo Armas overthrew the elected President, Jacobo Arbenz, and initiated that country's long and continuing agony. I was living in Guatemala at that time; it was there that I learned something of what it meant to be born and to live in Central America and the Caribbean. On the long boat-ride from Amsterdam, we had docked in Ciudad Trujillo, the then capital of the Dominican Republic. Fat rats climbed over the corrugated roofs of the scalding wharfs and Trujillo's police would not let us land because we were bound for "red" Guatemala.

In the then flourishing Casa de la Cultura of Guatemala City, I met exiles from all over the continent, from Trujillo's island, from Batista's Cuba, from Somoza's Nicaragua, from Rojas Pinilla's Colombia, from Pérez Jiménez's Venezuela. The grammatical possessive is, in this case, not simply a rhetorical device since these countries were fiefdoms whose dictators were usually maintained in power by U.S. support. Many of the exiles dreamed of an emancipated Latin America, as a place where a generous vision of social justice might eventually prevail. What in fact followed was the invasion of Guatemala (1954), of the Dominican Republic (1965), the Brazilian military coup (1964), the destabilization and overthrow of the Allende regime in Chile (1973), not to mention the more recent interventions in Grenada and Panama.

Ever since the Uruguayan critic, Enrique Rodó, published his *Ariel* in 1900, Latin Americans had tended to view the Mexican-American border as separating two rival versions of civilization. Two of Mir's great contemporaries, Pablo Neruda in his *Canto general* (1950) and Nicolás Guillén in *West Indies Ltd.* (1934), had also addressed themselves defiantly to the United States in order to affirm Latin American difference. The fact that Mir's work is less known than these has much to do with his place of birth, the Dominican Republic—whose literature still today is far less translated and disseminated than that of other Caribbean countries. It also has to do with his long exile from his homeland.

Mir's dialogue with Whitman belongs to a longstanding tradition. Whitman had been an icon to Latin Americans ever since the Cuban poet, José Martí, heard him speak in 1887, at what would be his last public appearance in New York. Martí's description fixed his image as a poet-prophet far above mere mortals. He wrote, "He [Whitman] seemed like a god last night, seated on a throne of red velvet, with his white hair, his beard falling on his chest, his eyebrows thick as a forest, his hand resting on a cane. . . ." Whitman's words, according to Martí, resembled the murmur of planets. But perhaps what most attracted Latin Americans, even those like Nicaragua's Rubén Darío who believed democracy to be at odds with art, was his American idiom and his claim to represent a New World.

Mir's poem is both a celebration of Whitman and an assertion of difference—a celebration of the poet of the common people and a denunciation of the "manifest destiny" of the nation that Whitman had helped to build. Whitman had brought together all the peoples of the United States into one choral and prophetic voice, "orotund, sweeping and final," and now it is the turn of people from outside those borders, the anonymous, marginalized inhabitants of Quisqueya, the Caribbean island which is now divided between the Dominican Republic and Haiti. Thus Mir both follows Whitman and diverges. He follows Whitman across a pristine America and identifies with its founding spirit, even with the Whitmanian *I* which, like a Leibnitzian monad, is "the revolving of all mirrors / around a single image." It is this self-affirmation that has given birth to the United States.

But here the two poets must diverge. Something has come between pure self-affirmation and fulfillment and that something is money, the simulacrum that replaces reality and which alienates human beings from the self. Mir here comes closest to Ernesto Cardenal's vision of a fallen humanity as he traces the degeneration of the Whitmanian *I* and its resurrection as imperial egoism that has commodified Latin America and deprived the nations of the continent of their autonomy. Whitman's spirit can only be redeemed by a new pronoun, the *we* of all those nations and peoples that have been "othered."

With the possible exception of Cardenal, few poets today would see Latin America's future with such self-confidence. For the times are different and poetry once again seems to be withdrawing from a civic function. Can the translation of such a poem do more than offer us a missing element of Latin America's past? Or can it during this difficult *fin de siècle* restore a tenuous hope—that the triumph of cynical reason may only be temporary?

Joint Tenants In Reality

~ Tammy Nuzzo-Morgan

The poetry of the good, gray bearded poet is so well-known worldwide that Long Islanders aren't the only ones to claim a piece of him as their own, yet people around the globe become Long Islanders by sharing Whitman's love of the "fish-shape Paumanok."

What follows are details that glimpse the "day to day" world of Whitman. Telling about these facts reveals how he was like us, *and* how we are indeed the sons and daughters of Whitman, though he (in the preface of his 1855 edition of *Leaves of Grass*) defined poets and readers as peers, joint tenants in reality.

Walter Whitman Sr. was of English heritage. He married Louisa Van Velsor in 1816. She was of Dutch and Welsh heritage.

Walter "Walt" Whitman, Jr. (5/31/1819 - 3/26/1892) was the second of eight children: the oldest, a brother, Jessie (1818-1870), himself, Mary (1822-1899), Hannah (1823-1908), Andrew Jackson (1827-1863), George Washington (1829-1901), Thomas Jefferson (1833-1890), and the youngest son, Edward (1835-1902), "Eddy", Walt's favorite, was mentally and physically handicapped. Eddy was institutionalized in 1881. Walt left the bulk of his estate to Eddy, that being $6000, his literary, and real property.

When Walt was eleven he was done with formal schooling and held his first paying job as an office boy for the law firm of James B. Clarke and his son Edward on lower Fulton Street in Brooklyn. While Walt ran errands for the law firm he was able to explore Brooklyn, known as the "city of churches."

Working for *The Long Island Patriot*, as an apprentice under the tutelage of Samuel E. Clement in 1831, was his next position. Walt used a hand press for printing the paper's single sheet of four pages.

During the Civil War Walt was a wound-dresser, an assistant that held the men down as they were having a limb sawed off, and a comforter that whispered that their darlings would still love them. He sometimes followed their bodies to the cemetery. Tending to the sick and wounded permanently undermined Walt's own health.

Walt greatly admired Abraham Lincoln. He wrote "O Captain! My Captain!" and "When Lilacs Last in the Dooryard Bloom'd" for him and gave annual lectures commemorating the death of the much loved president.

When Walt was in his early sixties he owned a yellow and white dog named "Tip" while he lived with his brother George and George's wife, Louisa. He was fond of singing in the tub, and didn't mind being late to dinner while he relaxed soaking and singing, even though his sister-in-law had called him several times to supper.

Walt bought his first home in 1884 at age 64, in Camden, New Jersey at 328 Mickle Street for $1750. He had to get a $500 loan from his publisher at the *Philadelphia Public Ledger*.

Whitman was aging and his friends were concerned for his physical and financial health, and so came up with the idea of The Lovering Bill in 1886. It was introduced by Congressman Henry B. Lovering of Lynn, Massachusetts. It was to award $25 a month to Whitman in recognition of his hospital work during the war. But the bill met with immediate anger of an old Boston enemy, Colonel Thomas Wentworth Higginson, a war hero who had commanded the Union's first black regiment. While the Colonel was recovering from a bout of seasickness during the Civil War is when he first met Whitman. Higginson considered Whitman a malingerer for hiding in the wards instead of fighting on the front lines. Whitman himself wasn't thrilled about the bill and doubted it would pass. He was correct, it didn't.

Another plan to help Whitman was put into action by Thomas Donaldson, a Philadelphia lawyer, who was an authority on American Indians. Whitman was known to suffer bad vertigo fits due to the heat, and having suffered a bad fall was in danger of declining into a shut-in. Donaldson sent out thirty-six letters describing his project and soliciting individual gifts of ten dollars. Mark Twain was one of those that contributed. Whitman cried when he saw the horse and buggy that was bought for him, which he named Phaeton: the young god that drove the chariot of the sun across the sky.

While some of Whitman's peers were kind, many were not. Emily

Dickinson called him disgraceful, Herman Melville said he never read Whitman's book, and even though Mark Twain gave the ten dollars, when asked by a Senate subcommittee on copyright to submit a list of American authors whose work should be protected he named only Cooper, Irving, Harriet Beecher Stowe, Poe, Emerson, William Dean Howells, and Thomas Bailey Aldrich.

One of the people responsible for the drafting of The Lovering Bill was Boston journalist Sylvester Baxter. While The Lovering Bill did not pass, Baxter did succeed in raising a subscription fund of eight-hundred dollars and gave it to Whitman in the summer of 1887. It was understood that Whitman would buy himself a second home, a little cottage in the country by the seashore. Whitman combined the "Summer Cottage Fund" with his savings and bought for himself his final resting place, a tomb in Harleigh Cemetery. He was laid to rest there after his death on March 26, 1892.

Poets Alfred Lord Tennyson and John Greenleaf Whittier also died that year. On January 1st, Ellis Island began accepting immigrants to the United States; January 15th, James Naismith published the rules for basketball; January 20th, at the YMCA in Springfield, Massachusetts, the first official basketball game was played; February 12th, Former President Abraham Lincoln's birthday was declared a national holiday; March 31st, the world's first fingerprinting bureau formally opened by the Buenos Aires Chief of Police; January to October, Benjamin Harrison was the president sitting in the White House, and in November, Grover Cleveland was elected.

Sources:
Walt Whitman: A Life by Justin Kaplan, New Republic Books, 1980.
<http://www.poets.org/poet.php/prmPID/126>
<http://www.poetseers.org/early_american_poets/walt_whitman/
   whitmans_poetry>
<http://www.whitmanarchive.org/>
<http://en.wikipedia.org/wiki/1892 >

~ ~ ~ ~ ~

A Forward Glance Towards Roads Un-traveled*

~ Annabelle Moseley

My first experience with Whitman, the Father of American Poetry, came when I was seven-years old, and was asked to recite, "O Captain! My Captain!" for a visiting writer who came to our school. I remember how much I liked the way the words felt in my mouth — how satisfying the mood and rhythm were. I was already convinced that I would be a poet, and I saw the way this poem moved the visiting writer, as it moved something in me. I was intrigued by Whitman's mystique.

Ten-years old, in fifth grade, I experienced a profound forward glimpse towards roads un-traveled while having an early taste of the life of a poet. I entered and won first place in the Walt Whitman Birthplace Association's annual poetry contest for children. I distinctly remember reading my poem, "The Colors of Long Island," at the awards celebration and meeting the great William Stafford, who was the Birthplace Association Poet-in-Residence that year. It was 1990. He would die three years later. Standing before the crowd and reading my poem made a huge impact on me— not simply because I was standing in front of Walt Whitman's birthplace (just a ten-minute drive from where I was growing up). I saw my father's face shining proudly in the crowd. My father, an English teacher, died less than a year after that event. His joy at seeing me read a poem in Walt's honor at Whitman's house, made me trust in later years that he caught a glimpse of my dream beginning to be fulfilled.

My prize that day was a modest savings bond, which I handed off to my parents. I was more interested in what the savings bond was tucked inside— a small Bantam Classic edition of *Leaves of Grass*. I began to read and savor it that summer and still have it with me— spine-weary, and riddled with footnotes and underlining in the pages within. That book represented a connection to the father of American poetry, and to my own father. It still does.

I trust that almost every writer within these leaves has a story of when they first connected with Walt Whitman's work— in a way that goes deeper than mere professional admiration— in a way that feels more like the loyalty of an apprentice to a master, of a child to a father. As a teacher, I enjoy seeing the look of delight and discovery on each of my young student's faces when they read Whitman aloud for the first time.

I like to show them how very often in *Leaves of Grass* Whitman addresses his reader directly— as though longing to reach out a hand through the yellowing pages of his green leaves. The poetry of Whitman makes each reader feel less alone. And for the lonely tendencies of many teenagers, and indeed, many poets… that is comfort indeed.

   poet's note:
* A play on Whitman's "A Backward Glance o'er Travel'd Roads"

Here is the poem I read that day in 1990:

The Colors of Long Island

If Long Island were a picture, how would I paint it?
I know the colors I would use.
Bright colors, that make the golden sunsets at Huntington Harbor.
Glistening white, for the foam of the great ocean at Fire Island
And the deep, white snow that makes winter
        Cozy when I sit by the fireside after sledding at Bald Hill.
Red, for the quaint farmhouses along the road to Orient Point.
Purple, for the lush vineyards at Cutchogue.
Beige, for the sand that tickles my toes as I frolic at Montauk.
Forest green, for the bountiful Pine Barrens of Brookhaven,
        Where we save its beauty for future generations.
Emerald green, for the trees at Sagamore Hill, that whisper
        And tell me secrets of the history there.
Turquoise, for the water at Sunken Meadow,
        One of my favorite places on the island.
The colors of Wedgwood blue, mustard gold, and barn red
        Cover historic houses and shops at Cold Spring Harbor.
I would use grey for the water at night on Jones Beach.
I would paint a silver moon shining its beams on the waves
        Like crystals, dancing to the music from some show there,
        Echoing in the air.
I would use golds and greens for the colors of Harvest.
Harvest is a busy time, on the farms in Riverhead.
Pastels of pink and lavender warm the gardens at Greenvale.
My brush would dabble rich browns and slate grey
        For the horses on the fields of Dix Hills.
But sadly, there is no canvas big enough to portray the variety
        And all the wonders of Long Island.
I was born here, I live here still, and I plan to stay here,
        Enjoying a colorful life on Long Island
        And doing all I can to brighten the painting…

    ~ Annabelle Moseley, age 10

≈ ≈ ≈ ≈ ≈

TELEGRAM FROM WALT WHITMAN:
The Long and Immense Road STOP Sing! STOP Be Free

~ Mankh

One's-Self I Sing

One's-Self I sing, a simple separate person,
Yet utter the word Democratic, the word En-Masse.

Of physiology from top to toe I sing,
Not physiognomy alone nor brain alone is worthy for the Muse,
    I say the Form complete is worthier far,
The Female equally with the Male I sing.

Of Life immense in passion, pulse, and power,
Cheerful, for freest action form'd under the laws divine,
The Modern Man I sing.

* * * * *

This first poem in *Leaves of Grass* is Whitman in a nutshell, his prime-directive, *raison d'etre*, guiding force, harbinger and bringer, both celebrating and honoring the individual as well as the whole, the body (every bit of it) as well as the mind, the spirit and soul, the male as well as the female, and both the male and female within each of us (thank you, Carl Jung!) yet all guided by "the laws divine." "Freest action" but not random or reckless! "Freest action" within holy and wholey and holey parameters. But Whitman in a nutshell?!

I confess, Whitman brings out the drama in me, goads me to thesauru-size (try to pronounce that!)-- and to expand upon what has just been written BECAUSE Whitman is as much about the FUN one has getting there as he is about the GETTING THERE.

There are open roads to meander and places to go but Whitman is no aimless fool, rather, he is well-balanced, well-versed, and ready to simply BE and reveal:

> *Stop this day and night with me and you shall possess the origin of all poems...*

Yes, the great rambler, who put his arms around America and squeezed so hard that many people got nervous, insulted or downright nasty, yes, this rambler knew how to

STOP

and talk, and smell the roses, the coffee, the perfume, his own arm-pits (of which he described the scent, "aroma finer than prayer").

So the questions begs: WHO is this man who claims to know *the origin of all poems*? And WHAT is the origin?

Walt Whitman has a Christ or Buddha or Lao Tzu or Fill-In-The-Blank-like stature for many poets and admirers. Unfortunately many misread him in a similar fashion that religions misread Christ and Buddha and so on; they (and he) were outside-the-box, free-spirits, not duplicateable though certainly fine examples of how to get on in the world. They are not to be copied or crucified or tarred-and-feathered (although Whitman actually was). As Bashô, a Master of haiku, wrote: "Do not follow in the footsteps of the old poets, seek what they sought."

Looking upon often turbulent US and world affairs, I'll borrow a modern cliché and ask: what would Whitman do?

Well, he would as suredly march in a Gay pride parade as attend a suburban yard sale as play in an office baseball game as visit the mall named after him in Huntingon as walk in a Peace March... C'mon, do you get it, America? Whitman was as much ahead of his time as he was in 'original time' which goes back to his line *Nature without check with original energy*. He went to the Source and brought it back in unfurling banners and ribbons of enthusiasm. Whitman knew what was before and what had been lost because he wanted it back again, anew... *give me again O Nature your primal sanities*!

And by "Nature" he didn't just mean habitat; he meant the true Nature of 'beings,' and living the Natural way, and staying connected with what is prime, first, original and sane. Doing so helps to repair and transcend what has been twisted and abused by egoic machinations.

Whitman was 'everyman' and woman and child and hired hand and on and on, and still is... if you read his poems. One thing, however, that I dislike about Whitman is that on occasion he lauds war, for example:

Give me...
The saloon of the steamer! the crowded excursion for me! the
*   torch-light procession!*
The dense brigade, bound for the war, with high piled military
*   wagons following...*

Some might read that as unabashed Whitmanesque enthusiasm for everything, but the question that comes to mind is: why *Give me?*...

STOP

As poet, Whitman is the master of the poetic run-on sentence, fashioning a new form to fit the times to capture AND release the American spirit. As Whitman in his day asked the questions *and* answered, so must each do in his/her time. Whitman's words from "A Backward Glance o'er Travel'd Roads":

   ...the New World needs the poems of realities and science and of the democratic average and basic equality, which shall be greater. In the centre of all, and object of all, stands the Human Being, towards whose heroic and spiritual evolution poems and everything directly or indirectly tend, Old World or New.

Perhaps this is a clue as to "the origin of all poems" — connect with the "heroic and spiritual evolution" of all beings!

Whitman went across America and around the globe on the flying carpet of his *Leaves of Grass* long before the Internet.

And what was Whitman's vision of America, his purpose for so embracing the country and the common man in his poetry? Again, his words:

   One main contrast of the ideas behind every page of my verses, compared with establish'd poems, is their different relative attitude towards God, towards the objective universe, and still more (by reflection, confession, assumption, &c.) the quite changed attitude of the ego, the one chanting or talking, towards himself and towards his fellow-humanity. It is certainly time for America, above all, to begin this readjustment in the scope and basic point of view of verse; for everything else has changed.

Whitman was heralding an awakening, a new day for a country still weaning, and a poetry and a voice that could carry all that. In "For You O Democracy" he writes:

I will plant companionship thick as trees all along the rivers of
    America, and along the shores of the great lakes, and all
    over the prairies...

        By the love of comrades,
          By the manly love of comrades.

For you these from me, O Democracy, to serve you ma femme!
For you, for you I am trilling these songs.

Whitman knew the Universe and all it contains is One ...*every atom belonging to me as good belongs to you.*

He is sage, guide, friend, and elder. One of my mantras for how-to-deal-with-the-modern-information-age comes from section 2 in *Song of Myself*:

You shall listen to all sides and filter them from your self.

Interestingly, he didn't write "for" your self, but "from." This hints at the Buddhist practice of "non-attachment" to worldly affairs and things. And the purpose of *that* is to nurture, grow into fullness, and maintain one's true Self. The "from" also suggests that by 'filtering' one may keep the bits that work... and discard the rest.

STOP

Stop this day and night with me and you shall possess the origin
    of all poems,
You shall possess the good of the earth and sun, (there are
    millions of suns left,)
You shall no longer take things at second or third hand, nor look
    through the eyes of the dead, nor feed on the spectres in books,
You shall not look through my eyes either, nor take things from me,
You shall listen to all sides and filter them from your self.

STOP

And touch upon Whitman's quieter, contemplative and intimate side, which is frequently overlooked in favor of his robust enthusiasm.

I lean and loafe at my ease observing a spear of summer grass.

How many of us do that nowadays?!

One of his shortest poems is delicate and confessional.

Here the Frailest Leaves of Me

Here the frailest leaves of me and yet my strongest lasting,
Here I shade my thoughts, I myself do not expose them,
And yet they expose me more than all my poems.

The first line is comparable to the Taoist idea that, what is new born and seemingly frail is truly full of life; the second line, speaks of humility and privacy; and the third, his truer self.

Whitman writes with universal eroticism and gentle intimacy in "Whoever You Are Holding Me Now in Hand," from the section *Calamus* whose poetic grouping shows his clearest celebration of love among men.

Here to put your lips upon mine, I permit you,
With the comrade's long-dwelling kiss or the new husband's kiss,
For I am the new husband and I am the comrade.

Or if you will, thrusting me beneath your clothing,
Where I may feel the throbs of your heart or rest upon your hip...

For all his mystical subtleties, it is still Whitman's *joie de vivre* that continues to spark the fires of writers and readers around the world.

Whitman is a time-traveler; he sought to make the page come alive. All the energy that Whitman put into the words is still there vibrating, and more excitedly when someone is holding the book. Think about that! Whitman told us: there is no separation and what you now read IS me in the flesh, can you feel me... though my physical body may have long turned to dirt?

So, I leave it to each reader to "filter" and decide whether Whitman was one or all or any of the following: a poet of vivid imagination, a literary original, a reincarnated holy man, a 19th century Messiah, an American Buddha, a Taoist, a holist, a mystic, horny-as-all-get-up, a true democrat, a jingoist, a revolutionary...

Whitman wrote, in "Are You the New Person Drawn toward Me?":

I am surely far different from what you suppose...

However one attempts to label him (if at all), quite simply: Walt Whitman has been around the cosmic block and then some, and is apparently still hovering... urging us to experience fully the timelessly brief moments of this *Life immense*, as well as to find out what *laws divine* really are so that we can live under and with them.

> *Long and long has the grass been growing,*
> *Long and long has the rain been falling,*
> *Long has the globe been rolling around.*
>
> from "Song of the Exposition"

∼ ∼ ∼ ∼ ∼

Holding Each Other's Hands

~ Geraldine Green 3 September 2006

I got to know Walt Whitman when I was 27, a photographer friend introduced me to *Leaves of Grass*. I'd never written poetry before, only kept a journal, which I called my 'red file', for three years. He read it and said, "look, you have that same kind of bounding energy and joy in life and people that Walt Whitman has"... so, thanks, my friend, for making me acquainted with Walt's poetry.

His photo in front of me -- here in Cumbria, England -- I got it from the Walt Whitman Museum at West Hills in July, he's looking me right in the eye, with a kind of jaunty glance, his hand firmly on his hip, knuckles digging into his thigh, hat, wide-brimmed on one side, slouching with his hand in his pocket, ready to take out a leaf, pebble, button, a find to give me from his travels. I sat on the porch of his home, where he was born into this world from the birthing bed in the back room, thick twined mattress, with a wooden peg that tightens the strings and from which grew the saying "night night, sleep tight, watch the bed bugs don't bite!" – the sleep tight bit is here's hoping the strings have been tightened!

He was born on Long Island in 1819, but this isn't going to be a history lesson, you can get that from websearching or books, this is my friendship with the man, what I know of his poems and what he's given to me, stretching from America in the 19th century to Cumbria, England right here and now in the 21st. Because the man was about what it is to be alive, to wake each morning and sniff each new dawn, to lay awake as we might do, wherever we are, at night and listen to owls calling, sheep bleating, the Long Island Railroad train's mournful hooting or trucks, traffic, cows, people, birds, motorbikes, sirens and children. It's about the rain here and now on my windows, the taste of grilled sausages in my mouth, my fingers on these keys and my feet feeling the first slight cool breeze of autumn, coming from the open bathroom window.

Let me open *The Complete Poems of Walt Whitman* (introduction by David Rogers, Wordsworth Press, 1995) and let's settle down in the moment, wherever you are reading this, Walt, come along and share this friendly morning chat, not on the front porch of your lilac-sprayed house, but here in my little study, looking out onto Skiddaw, or with friends around the world, sitting in their front rooms, standing on a train on their way to work, or in a library maybe, hearing themselves breathe:

I DREAM'D IN A DREAM

I dream'd in a dream I saw a city invincible to the attacks of
    the whole of the rest of the earth,
I dream'd that was the new city of Friends,
Nothing was greater there than the quality of robust love, it led
    the rest,
It was seen every hour in the actions of the men of that city,
And in all their looks and words.

(from Calamus)

and here's a picture of your house, in the shadow of trees, its clapboard walls merging with the dappled light and shade, a long old fence dividing maybe garden from field but not your spirit, your spirit wasn't separate from the next man or woman or child's, nor was it separate from the earth's, the leaves sun wind rain and newly built dreams of a hopeful nation.

I celebrate myself, and sing myself,
And what I assume you shall assume,
For every atom belonging to me as good belongs to you.

I loafe and invite my soul,
I lean and loafe at my ease observing a spear of summer grass.

(from Song of Myself)

We need the perfume of his singing more than ever today in a world crazy with fear and greed, we need his soaring spirit to allow us to fly again in hope and joy at the blazing sun lighting up a spear of grass, let our green juices rise with ease and let us loafe together wherever we find ourselves, full of 'robust love' as we invite the earth to,

Smile O voluptuous cool-breathed earth!
Earth of the slumbering and liquid trees!
Earth of departed sunset—earth of the mountains misty-topt!
Earth of the vitreous pour of the full moon and just tinged with blue!
Earth of shine and dark mottling the tide of the river!
Earth of the limpid gray of clouds brighter and clearer for my sake!
Far-swooping elbowed earth—rich apple-blossomed earth!
Smile, for your lover comes.

(from Song of Myself)

By reading this book you let Walt's hand and mine be there with you... holding each other's hands in a never-ending dance through time and space, from the fierce vibrancy of cave paintings our ancestors drew of animals and birds they shared the earth with, to where we are now, each of us having the potential to sing our own songs as we try and create a happier universe together.

≈ ≈ ≈ ≈ ≈

Walt Whitman's Natural Resources

~ Maxwell Corydon Wheat, Jr.

Having studied the mocking-bird's tones and the flight of the
   mountain-hawk,
And heard at dawn the unrivall'd one,
   the hermit thrush from the swamp-cedars,
Solitary, singing in the West, I strike up for a New World.
                              from "Starting from Paumanok"
                              ~ Walt Whitman

These are natural resources — the "delicious gurgles, crackles, screams, weeps,"[1] of the mockingbird, the swoop of the hawk and the "pure deliberate notes"[2] of the Hermit Thrush. In the "dust-bowl" era of textbook conservation, we learned about natural resources in terms of land being blown away in the wind out west or mining for coal and ores and harvesting crops and fish — all very important. But in our increasing crowded and concreted civilization, there is growing — perhaps desperate — awareness of the natural resources for the spiritual and artistic.

Indeed, all nature "Of earth, rocks, Fifth-month flowers experienced, stars, rain, snow,"[3] are used by many poets for much of their imagery and expression.

Solitary the thrush,
The hermit withdrawn to himself,
   avoiding the settlements
Sings by himself a song.[4]

What indeed are the words that express overwhelming tides of joy and grief; or articulate the obscure, the ambiguous, the enigmatical that permeates feelings deeply psychological and spiritual? How does the artist translate subtlety, poignancy, and ecstasy?

Haven't you read — or have even heard "live" through television or radio — the astronauts' attempts to express their wonder. "What a beautiful view!"[5] exclaimed Commander Alan Shepard, America's first man in space. "Can see clear back to a big cloud pattern back across the Cape. Beautiful sight,"[6] reported Colonel John Glenn. Hardly "language charged with meaning to the utmost possible degree,"[7] Ezra Pound would surely agree.

I recall the television and radio news commentator Frank McGee saying a few years ago that someday a poet-astronaut should be hoisted off that launching pad in Cape Kennedy. For McGee was asserting that only a poet could find the words to describe the new combinations of view and emotion being experienced by our weight-less globe-circling men. (And now moon-circling.) But the poet would probably have to utilize some more earth-orientated experiences of men to effect the fresh imagery and meaning.

T.S. Eliot suggests the formula when he asserts that no emotion can be expressed accurately in art without what he calls an "objective correlative . . . a set of objects, a situation, a chain of events which shall be the formula of that *particular* emotion; such that, when the external facts, which must terminate in sensory experience, are given, the emotion is immediately evoked."

Nature is a natural resource for the objective correlative. A Hermit Thrush singing in the white cedar swamps in the Pine Barrens region of Long Island was Whitman's objective correlative for his expression of grief for Lincoln.

One's mood response to the sounds and sights of nature perhaps depends on the person's psychological orientation at the time. Yet, it is phenomenal how often the Hermit Thrush song is reported in terms of loneliness, plaintiveness — "the cool, lonely meditation of the hermit thrush in the depths of the woods"[8] says drama critic Brooks Atkinson in *Once Around the Sun*.

Because of his known walks and enjoyment of Long Island nature we can feel fairly certain that Whitman was well aware of the Hermit Thrush in the Island's pine barrens and cedar swamps — that perhaps he had actually heard it there. It would fit into the context of his overall interest and awareness of nature. This context explains many of his uses — of the Yellow-crowned Heron which would probably go unnoticed by the casual sojourner in the coastal wetlands. In *Song of Myself* he refers to:

Where the yellow-crown'd heron comes to the edge of the
   marsh at night and feeds upon small crabs...[9]

Whitman writes in his prose in *Specimen Days:*

Did you ever chance to hear the midnight flight of birds passing through the air and darkness overhead, in countless armies, changing their early summer habitat? It is something not to be forgotten. A friend called me up just after 12 last night to mark the peculiar noise of unusually immense flocks migrating north (rather late this year). In the silence, shadow and delicious odor of the hour, (the natural perfume belonging to the night alone,) I thought it rare music. You could hear the characteristic motion — once or twice the 'rush of mighty wings,' but oftener a velvety rustle, long drawn out — sometimes quite near — with continual calls and chirps, and some songnotes. It all lasted from 12 till after 2. Once in a while the species was plainly distinguishable; I could make out the the bobolink, tanager, Wilson's thrush, white crown'd sparrow, and occasionally from high in the air came the notes of the plover.[10]

From Whitman's own admissions, one can perhaps sometimes question his identifications. But it's the observations — of behavior, for example — that count. He "had studied the mocking-bird's tones."

I was suddenly and excitedly aware of this at about one o'clock on a spring morning when a couple of Mockingbirds were singing across some backyards in the suburbs of Baltimore, Maryland where I was visiting relatives. Between the sounds of cardinals, caged canaries and spring peepers, plus a variety of generous chirps and workman-like calls, it occurred to me that these birds seemed to be answering each other across the space of these few backyards. Although there was some overlapping, one would usually hold forth alone — with the other, when it commenced, picking up some of the final notes of its colleague. Then spontaneously there occurred to me a line from "Out of the Cradle Endlessly Rocking" that I had wondered about but never could adequately explain — "musical shuttle."

Out of the cradle endlessly rocking
Out of the mocking-bird's throat, the musical shuttle...

It was an uncanny feeling to believe that I was hearing essentially the same kind of performance that Whitman might once have listened to very closely.

I would suggest that today's artist looking ahead in the 21st century ponder Whitman and what he means about a "New World."

footnotes: [All poetic quotes of Whitman fr. The Poetry and Prose of Walt Whitman, edited by Louis Untermeyer and publ. by Simon and Schuster, N.Y. 1949]

1. "Song of Myself", section 33
2. "When Lilacs Last in the Dooryard Bloom'd", section 15
3. "Starting from Paumanok", section 1
4. "When Lilacs Last in the Dooryard Bloom'd", section 4
5. Shelton, William Roy, <u>American Space Exploration</u>. Little, Brown & Co. Boston, Mass. 1967. Page 149
6. Ibid., page 200
7. Pound, Ezra, <u>ABC of Reading</u>, New Directions Books, N.Y., 1960. Page 36
8. Atkinson, Brooks. <u>Once Around the Sun</u>, Harcourt, Brace & Co., N.Y. 1951. Page 179
9. "Song of Myself", section 33
10. Whitman, Walt. <u>The Poetry and Prose of Walt Whitman</u>, Louis Untermeyer, editor, Simon and Schuster, NY, 1949. Page 673

≈ ≈ ≈ ≈ ≈

Poets to Come:
Teaching Whitman in High School

~ Bill Zavatsky

My first sustained reading of Walt Whitman took place in the fall of 1965 or the spring of 1966. It was his *Song of Myself*, a good chunk of which I read while sitting in a lobby at the New School for Social Research in New York, waiting for a jazz improvisation class to begin. After three years at a small college in Connecticut, I had "dropped out" and worked for a year. When I resumed my education after having transferred to Columbia, I felt myself at a new beginning. Whitman confirmed my adventure—the new life on which I had embarked as well as the stirrings of a real commitment to writing, especially to poetry. That afternoon, at the New School, Whitman's rolling line fused itself to the long-lined solos of the jazz artists that I most admired; and all I had to do was look around me to see that he was one of the great poets of New York.

But more than this, Whitman's work touched experiences in me that had long been buried, experiences the nature of which I can only call spiritual. Some years ago, when I started teaching his poems to my tenth- and twelfth-grade English classes, I turned to Whitman because he was one of those writers who confirmed a sensation that, up through my teens, I had now and again felt: the gift of seeing everything in my range of vision with a startling clarity, as if whatever I turned my gaze toward was bathed in the beam of a powerful searchlight, but not at the expense of surrounding objects, which retained their focus. Concomitant with this heightened sense of vision was the sensation of being connected to all that I saw, joined to it in a oneness that both dazzled me and left me with a feeling of inner joy.

These states did not last very long, and they were so extraordinary that I was afraid to investigate them, even to mention them. (They seemed qualitatively *different* from the feelings of piety or devotion or exaltation that I experienced as a Roman Catholic boy.) The manifestation was not linked to creed or dogma, but showered down upon me when I least expected it—on a spectacularly clear fall day, or a summer afternoon as I walked down a tree-lined street, heading home from a baseball game. All I knew was that they "happened," that I was grateful for these visitations, and that I would remember the effect that they had had upon me. Now every year I teach Whitman to my "Poets to Come," the future generation of writers that he addressed in his short poem of that name. I preface our reading of his work by describing the experiences that I have just related. There is a hunger in young people—"religious" or not—to discuss "heightened" transpersonal experiences. In doing so I never feel that I am forcing a belief system on my students. For example, as I gave my little personal introduction on the first day of our Whitman studies, two female seniors were madly scribbling notes to one another. With a frown, but really out of curiosity, I walked over to read what one of them had written: "I have these experiences all the time!" Her friend had responded enthusiastically in the affirmative. The encounter made me realize that Whitman is one of the perfect companions for an adolescent who is open to the world and the host of experiences that it offers to us.

There are higher levels of spirituality in poetry than the writings of Whitman—the poems of William Blake or Hindu texts like the *Bhagavad-Gita*—but at present these seem out of my own teaching range despite my absorption in them. What Whitman seemed to have experienced, however, was far more profound than my own little moments of transport. What especially appealed to me was Whitman's directness, the sense that he was speaking from the heart of a great mystery in a language that I could understand. Neither I nor my students need to cut through a lot of cultural differences and symbol-systems to understand Whitman, and this is what I wanted to explore and to communicate to them: an apprehension of spiritual matters that was immediate. Not that everything in his work is transparent; the studies of what Whitman meant in *Song of Myself* are still tumbling off the presses. I wanted the excuse at least to touch on spiritual things, and Whitman supplied the occasion.

Of course, all poetry is spiritual to a greater or lesser extent. Whitman himself wrote:

Much is said of what is spiritual, and of spirituality, in this, that, or the other—in objects, expressions.—For me, I see no object, no expression, no animal, no tree, no art, no book, but I see, from morning to night, and from night to morning, the spiritual.—Bodies are all spiritual.—All words are spiritual—nothing is more spiritual than words (*An American Primer*, 1).

In Class

After I had told the story of my youthful "experiences" and read aloud the passages from *Song of Myself* quoted in the first item of the following list, my classes and I used the chalkboard to make a grand list of the features that seemed to be characteristic of Whitman's poems. (My seniors had already read *Song of Myself*, "The Sleepers," "Faces," and "I Sing the Body Electric" from the 1855 text of *Leaves of Grass*; my sophomores read the final edition of the *Song* and "Out of the Cradle Endlessly Rocking" in *The Mentor Book of Major American Poets*.) Here's our list of the qualities that we found in Whitman:

1. *Spirituality*: By which is meant an appeal to or manifestation of transcendence; an understanding that each individual is identical with the One. Everywhere in his work, but most notably in *Song of Myself*, Whitman refers to the central fact of his life, the spiritual experience which he evidently had sometime in the early 1850s, first memorialized in section 5 of *Song of Myself*:

I believe in you my soul . . . . the other I am must not abase itself to you,
And you must not be abased to the other.
. . .
I mind how we lay in June, such a transparent summer morning;
You settled your head athwart my hips and gently turned over upon me,
And parted the shirt from my bosom-bone, and plunged your tongue to my
    barestript heart,
And reached till you felt my beard, and reached till you held my feet.

Swiftly arose and spread around me the peace and joy and knowledge that
    pass all the art and argument of the earth;
And I know that the hand of God is the elderhand of my own,
And I know that the spirit of God is the eldest brother of my own,
And that all the men ever born are also my brothers . . . . and the women my
    sisters and lovers,
And that a kelson of the creation is love;
And limitless are leaves stiff or drooping in the fields,
And brown ants in the little wells beneath them,
And mossy scabs of the wormfence, and heaped stones, and elder and mullein
    and poke-weed. (ll. 73-74, 78-89)

And in section 7 he returns to it:

Has any one supposed it lucky to be born?
I hasten to inform him or her it is just as lucky to die, and I know it.
I pass death with the dying, and birth with the new-washed babe . . . . and am
    not contained between my hat and boots.

And peruse manifold objects, no two alike, and every one good,
The earth good, and the stars good, and their adjuncts all good.

I am not an earth nor an adjunct of an earth,
I am the mate and companion of people, all just as immortal and fathomless as myself;
They do not know how immortal, but I know. (ll. 122-129)

The erotic language of the first description is perfectly consistent with the narratives of saints and mystics. Relative to the piercing of the heart imagery in part 5 (see above), we read Saint Teresa's account of being pierced with a spear by an angel. (See the J.M. Cohen translation of *The Life of Saint Teresa of Ávila by Herself* [Penguin Books, 210-11].) We likewise examine a reproduction of Bernini's famous sculpture based on this passage for a better understanding of what Whitman may be suggesting. We also read selections from the poetry of Kabir, Rumi, and St. John of the Cross, all of whom speak of God as their "lover."

2. *Emphasis on the physical body*: That the body is good, clean, pure. "Welcome is every organ and attribute of me, and of any man hearty and clean,/ Not an inch nor a particle of an inch is vile, and none shall be less familiar than the rest" (ll. 49-50).

3. *Celebration/praise*: All of creation is good and worthy of praise. Kenneth Koch and Kate Farrell mention that the *Song of Myself* is an "exuberant inventory of the world (and so of Walt Whitman) in which he congratulates and praises all the parts of life in great detail, and all for just existing" (*Sleeping on the Wing*, 37).

4. *Love for all things, whether "good" or "evil"*— a repudiation of duality, which is merely the misreading of a unified principle, since the unenlightened human mind is incapable of grasping the One. Furthermore, the compassion that we find everywhere expressed in Whitman's writing may be seen as a form of imagination, allowing us to feel what others are feeling. (For this last idea see part 11, "Twenty-eight young men bathe by the shore" (ll. 193-210.)

5. *Equality*: of all humans; also, there is more than a hint in Whitman that the processes of nature exist on a par with human life. Section 32 begins, "I think I could turn and live awhile with the animals . . . . they are so placid and self contained,/ I stand and look at them sometimes half the day long" (ll. 684-685).

6. *Emphasis on the Present Tense*: Another technique that Whitman uses to generate the feeling of "eternity" and immediacy in many of his greatest poems is to keep to the present tense. In *Song of Myself* the present tense dominates the action.

7. *The list or catalog*: Whitman's lists "level" everything, thus making everything equal. This is to say that finally, in his lists, nothing takes precedence over another thing, and nothing comes first or last. The notion of the democratic—another key idea in Whitman's work—abides in such a conception.

8. *The simultaneity of the list*: Chains of events happening at once result in a feeling of timelessness. The poet is thus godlike, standing at the center of time, able to see and feel all things at once. Also, the poet tends to disappear into his enumerations, a technique that heightens the feeling of spirituality, of Oneness, calling to the detachment from ego. Simultaneity also creates a sense of movement, often of speed, in the text.

9. *Repetition*: A phenomenon of the list. It creates an incantatory feeling that approaches the rhythms of the prayer or chant, also heightening the sense of the spiritual. A discussion of Whitman's use of rhetorical devices such as anaphora (the repetition of the same word or words at the *beginning* of a line), epistrophe (the repetition of the same word or words at the *end* of a line), symploce (the combination of anaphora and epistrophe), and syntactical parallelism can sharpen the students' understanding of Whitman's poetic technique. These devices literally "make" his meaning. It's also important to remember that, in giving up rhyme and a regular meter, Whitman used the devices described above as substitutions for rhyme. Repetition, of course, generates meters of its own.

10. *Highly physical description alternating with abstract spiritual musings*: Whitman gains a tremendous power in his work because he continually buttresses his spiritual insights with concrete particulars (observed facts), and vice versa. Again, see part five of *Song of Myself*, which moves from the revelation of the summer morning to "the pace and joy and knowledge that pass all the art and argument of the earth" (l. 82) and back to physical details like "leaves stiff or drooping in the fields" (l. 87).

11. *Sexuality*: Whitman does not shy away from expressions of sexuality; this connects several of the above categories in our list—spirituality,

equality, democracy, physical description, love, celebration, and, of course, eroticism.

12. *Fearless use of the first person pronoun*: Whitman never shies away from using the word "I." *Song of Myself* begins with it ("I celebrate myself") and ends with it ("I stop somewhere waiting for you"). The constant use of the I is another element that creates the instantaneous intimacy of Whitman's voice.

13. *Intimacy of address*: The voice of Whitman is warm, friendly, encouraging, sometimes even animated by the fearlessness found in face-to-face conversation. He addresses the reader directly, creating a sense of closeness rare in poetry. (See Stephen Railton's excellent essay, "'As If I Were With You,'—The Performance of Whitman's Poetry," on Whitman's use of "you" in *The Cambridge Companion to Whitman* [7-26].)

14. *Individuality*: Despite the tendency of catalog poetry to "dissolve" the author's identity, his or her individual personality persists by virtue of the literary choices made and the style adopted. (The students and I were forced to acknowledge a paradoxical element here: to know that one is an individual and at the same time one with the Whole.)

15. *Adoption of Personae*: Whitman is fond of wearing masks in his poetry. For example, he assumes a variety of identities in part 10 of the *Song*: hunter, seafarer, clamdigger, witness of a marriage between a trapper and his Indian bride, protector of a runaway slave.

16. *"And to die is different from what any one supposed, and luckier"*: This line concludes and summarizes section 6, which begins with the famous opening, "A child said, What is the grass? fetching it to me with full hands" (6.1). The realization of individual death is transcended by the understanding that the soul is immortal.

17. *Natural diction spiced with "poetic" diction*: Whitman's sound—his choice of words—is very close to ours, very "modern." The "everydayness" of his vocabulary reflects the common sights and sounds that he celebrates. Whitman's language is also highly concrete and sensual, as if it could be grabbed and held before the eyes and felt with the hand. At the same time, we note that his use of certain words and expressions (sometimes from the French, especially in the poems after 1855) may be a bit off-putting: "venerealee" for one afflicted with venereal disease;

"amies" for "female friends"; "chef-d'oeuvre" for "masterpiece"; "ambulanza" for "ambulance"; "eleves" for "students"; "bussing" for "kissing," etc.

18. *A poet of the city*: Whitman was the first great poet to write of New York City, which connects to

19. *The poet as reporter*: For many years Whitman worked as a newspaperman. He went out into the streets, using his eyes and ears to gather facts—sights, sounds, smells, textures—that create the fabric of his writing. This technique was to lay the foundation for everything that he would write. In short, observation—the merging of one's sensibility with one's surroundings—is another way of being-at-one with the "other." It is a form of meditation, and thus intersects many of these other categories. That Whitman stands as a witness to his times is a hallmark of his work.

20. *The poet as storyteller*: There are anecdotes and short narratives throughout Whitman's long poems, especially in *Song of Myself* and "The Sleepers," even though these poems are thought of as non-narrative works. "The subject was so large that anything, it seemed, could be part of it and could be included" (Koch and Farrell, *Sleeping on the Wing*, 37).

21. *"Participle-loving Whitman"*: Here is the first stanza of "The Sleepers," in which I have emphasized the present participles by placing them in italics:

I wander all night in my vision,
Stepping with light feet . . . . swiftly and noiselessly *stepping* and *stopping*,
Bending with open eyes over the shut eyes of sleepers;
Wandering and confused . . . . lost to myself . . . . ill-assorted . . . . contradictory,
Pausing and *gazing* and *bending* and *stopping*. (ll. 1-5)

The present participle stretches action by virtue of its elastic ending. It suggests action in the process of completion, but not yet finished, and implies (like so many of Whitman's techniques) the eternal present and the Eternal. It is a technique that must be used carefully; otherwise it can succumb to the greeting-card effect of "soft" poetry. See Ezra Greenspan's enlightening article on Whitman's use of this part of speech in *The Cambridge Companion to Walt Whitman* (92-109).

22. *Frequent and unusual use of the ellipsis (. . . .)*: Particularly odd in nineteenth-century poetry. This piece of punctuation is Whitman's hieroglyph for the drawn breath, the pause for thought, the opening-up of the poem into timelessness, the intrusion of the eternal into consciousness whenever we leave off speaking—that is, when the individual ego is adumbrated. At the end of a poem the ellipsis usually means something like, "I have nothing more to say." In Whitman it means something different: a unit of breath; little stars or planets rolling by. . . . (Whitman struck out the ellipses in editions of *Leaves of Grass* that appeared after 1855.)

23. *The long line*: Whitman's long lines contain or generate many of the above qualities. His line is a rolling wave, an oceanic motion; a planetary orbit; the process of drawing and exhaling breath—as a focus in meditation. (The long line also testifies to Whitman's devotion to opera.)

The origin of Whitman's line in Biblical literature seems evident. Here is a passage from the Old Testament (which I have arranged into verse lines) that contains the seed of Whitman's major theme in *Song of Myself*:

Comfort ye, comfort ye my people, saith your God.
Speak ye comfortably to Jerusalem, and cry unto her, that her warfare is
    accomplished, that her iniquity is pardoned: for she hath received of the
    Lord's hand double for all her sins.
The voice of him that crieth in the wilderness,
Prepare ye the way of the Lord, make straight in the desert a highway for our
    God.
Every valley shall be exalted, and every mountain and hill shall be made low:
    and the crooked shall be made straight, and the rough places plain:
And the glory of the Lord shall be revealed, and all flesh shall see it together:
    for the mouth of the Lord hath spoken it.
The voice said, Cry. And he said, What shall I cry? All flesh is grass, and all the
    goodliness thereof is as the flower of the field:
The grass withereth, the flower fadeth: because the spirit of the Lord bloweth
    upon it: surely the people is grass.
The grass withereth, the flower fadeth: but the word of our God shall stand for
    ever. (Isaiah 40:1-8, King James Version)

The voice of God speaks through the mouth of the prophet, and Whitman himself for a time thought of his book as a "new Bible" for the American masses. Grass recurs as a life-image throughout literature and mythology. The Oglala Sioux holy man Black Elk, at the beginning of his autobiography, says: "So many other men have lived and shall live that story [of an individual life], to be grass upon the hills" (*Black Elk Speaks*, 1; my interpolation in brackets). We grow, flourish, and die (for a time) like blades of grass. Whitman's title suggests the leaves (pages) of a book, at once eternal and transitory. We can also imagine a book printed on blades of grass, each blade being the page of the book of eternity. Guy Davenport notes that "this one universal plant [is] absent only in the deserts of the poles," and that "the first paper was leaves of grass, papyrus" (Davenport, 76). Hence Whitman's description of it as a "uniform hieroglyphic." Grass, tenacious and ubiquitous, is also a perfect symbol for democracy. (Again note that Whitman's image is ambiguous: the grass may need deciphering, but it is also universal, accessible to all.)

Naturally there is much more to be said on all these subjects, and there are plenty of further insights attendant on a close reading of Whitman. My students and I arrived at these ideas in one class session of "brainstorming," and I offer them as points of departure for further discussion. Use them as best suits your purpose.

Bibliography

Davenport, Guy. "Whitman" in *The Geography of the Imagination: Forty Essays* (San Francisco: North Point Press, 1981). A beautifully written and insightful essay: "[Whitman] closed the widening distance between poet and audience. He talks to us face to face, so that our choice is between listening and turning away. And in turning away there is the uneasy feeling that we are turning our backs on the very stars and on ourselves" (70). "Whitman's fond gaze was for grace that is unaware of itself; his constant pointing to beauty in common robust people was a discovery. Custom said that beauty was elsewhere" (71).

Greenspan, Ezra. *The Cambridge Companion to Walt Whitman* (Cambridge and New York: Cambridge University Press, 1995). Contains a number of solid essays about Whitman's life and writings. My personal favorite is Greenspan's "Some Remarks on the Poetics of 'Participle-Loving Whitman,'" which discusses one of Whitman's favorite stylistic devices.

Koch, Kenneth, and Kate Farrell. *Sleeping on the Wing: An Anthology of Modern Poetry with Essays on Reading and Writing* (New York: Random House, 1981; Vintage Books, 1982).

Neihardt, John G. *Black Elk Speaks: Being the Life Story of a Holy Man of the Oglala Sioux* (Lincoln, Nebraska: University of Nebraska Press, 1961;

originally published in 1932). A new edition of this book was published in paperback in 2001, with added notes, a useful map, and new introductory material.

Whitman, Walt. *Leaves of Grass: The First (1855) Edition*. Edited, with an introduction, by Malcolm Cowley (New York: Penguin Books, 1986; originally published in 1959). Cowley's excellent introduction makes as much sense out of the "structure" of Whitman's amorphous *Song of Myself* as any critic has. The virtue of this edition is that it gives us, with line numbers, the texts of important Whitman poems in their first and purest state. Unfortunately there are no explanatory notes to the poems, and Viking Penguin should get on the ball and commission someone to write them. There are too many odd vocabulary words and idiosyncratic usages for a high school student (even a college student) to cut through. (For those who might want a more durable version of this book, a hardcover edition is published by Barnes and Noble.)

_____. *An American Primer: With Facsimiles of the Original Manuscript*. Edited by Horace Traubel (San Francisco: City Lights Books, 1970; reprinted Duluth, MN: Holy Cow! Press, 1987; originally published in 1904).

≈ ≈ ≈ ≈ ≈

Shopping for Inspiration
(a revised version of an essay written as a student of Mr. Zavatsky - 10th grade)

~ Ali Lebow

In "A Supermarket in California," Allen Ginsberg creates a dark and lonely setting in which he seems uncomfortable and uninspired. Yet, he explores a new world of imagination where he is on a quest for inspiration. "A Supermarket in California" could be considered a discrete apostrophe poem. Ginsberg is talking to Walt Whitman while he also asks Garcia Lorca, "what were you doing down by the watermelons?"

It is a free verse poem filled with symbolism. Ginsberg is searching for inspiration which he metaphorically says is like shopping at an absurd supermarket, all the while comparing his writing style and personality to Walt Whitman.

Ginsberg mentions these two famous poets, Whitman and Garcia Lorca, both of whom were not alive on this earth when the poem was written. Ginsberg sees these two poets in his supermarket. He briefly mentions Lorca, who wrote an "Ode to Walt Whitman," while he focuses on Whitman.

Whitman wrote about America as a whole. Here, Ginsberg writes about how America, or as he calls it "the lost America," is changing, mentioning "whole families shopping at night!" Ginsberg sees these kinds of changes as revolutionary. Whole families shopping together is also an example of how Ginsberg sees America as a whole. Another example of this is when he mentions "blue automobiles in driveways."

Ginsberg also compares not only his writing but his personality to Whitman. He writes about how they walk together all night "through solitary streets." He says that both of them will be lonely. The cause of this loneliness may be because of another personality trait shared not only between Ginsberg and Whitman, but also with Lorca. All three of these poets faced the hardships of growing up at a time when it was not socially acceptable to be attracted to the same sex. The author says that he is constantly thinking about Whitman and in this dream-like poem he seems to be fantasizing about a relationship with him. A big clue that hints to Whitman's homosexuality is that Ginsberg mentions Whitman looking with interest at the grocery boys. In this poem, Ginsberg is not only shopping for ideas and inspiration, but also love.

~ ~ ~ ~ ~

Virginia Tech
and Our Need for a Poetic Language of Mourning

~ Maxwell Corydon Wheat, Jr.

America needs a reserve of poetic language to draw from for times of national grief. Language about people in America's cities and towns, language of the American countryside, its forests, prairies and farmyards, language about the song of the Hermit Thrush with which Walt Whitman sings his "carol . . . Death's outlet song of life. . ." for Abraham Lincoln in his grieving poem, "When Lilacs Last in the Dooryard Bloom'd." This is a poem that can be brought forth for mourning a national personage as it was for President John Kennedy. The Virginia Tech massacre, April 16th, 2007, also calls for a national poem.

For writing a poem about the 32 students and professors who were murdered by a deranged student, or about the Iraq War, the Katrina hurricane, floods or fires, "When Lilacs Last in the Dooryard Bloom'd" is a model for structure and choice of language. An eight or nine page (depending on font size) elegy, it consists of 16 numbered sections each of which, or a stanza or stanzas of each, can function as an individual poem and serve as a model for creating short poems expressing grief for Virginia Tech's lost or other mourning needs.

"When Lilacs Last in the Dooryard Bloom'd" is, among other genres, a processional poem passing across the pages like the black-draped presidential funeral train of nine cars traveling through the towns and over the countrysides for 1,662 miles from Washington to Springfield, Illinois. The first stanza, like a train's engine, stoked up from the poet's emotions fueled by his dwelling on "the great star drooped in the western sky in the night," (the bright planet Venus setting in the evening sky over Washington that Good Friday, April 14, 1865), pulls the cars and caboose of stanzas over the pages as if they were running on tracks, the caboose consisting of ritual closing lines "lilac and star and bird twined with the chant of my soul,/ There in the fragrant pines and the cedars dusk and dim." As Gay Wilson Allen and Charles T. Davis, editors of the book, *Whitman's Poems* published in 1955 by New York University Press, write, "The coffin has now reached the end of its journey and come to rest in 'the fragrant pines and the cedars dusk and dim.' "

Also, Sections 5 and 6 can each be experienced as a processional poem describing the train's journey, or both together can serve as a processional poem. Section 5 reads as follows:

Over the breast of the spring, the land, amid cities,
Amid lanes and through old woods, where lately the violets peep'd
    from the ground, spotting the grey debris,
Amid the grass in the fields each side of the lanes, passing the endless grass,
Passing the yellow-spear'd wheat, every grain from its shroud
    in the dark-brown fields uprisen,
Passing the apple-tree blows of white and pink in the orchards,
Carrying a corpse to where it shall rest in the grave,
Night and day journeys a coffin.

That is a model for a short processional poem. So is Section 6:

Coffin that passes through lanes and streets,
Through day and night with the great cloud darkening the land,
With the pomp of the inloop'd flags with the cities draped in black,
With the show of the States themselves as of crape-veil'd women standing,
With processions long and winding and the flambeaus of the night,
With the countless torches lit, with the silent sea of faces and the unbared
    heads,
With the waiting depot, the arriving coffin, and the sombre faces,
With dirges through the night, with the thousand voices rising strong and
    solemn,
With all the mournful voices of the dirges pour'd around the coffin,
The dim-lit churches and the shuddering organs—where amid these you
    journey,
With the tolling tolling bells' perpetual clang,
Here, coffin that slowly passes,
I give you my sprig of lilac.

Because "When Lilacs Last in the Dooryard Bloom'd" is a processional poem it works as a ritual poem. The word "processional" has a religious connotation, services usually incorporating at least one processional. The structure of a Whitmanesque ritual poem is that of any short poem (Lead, Build-up and Ending, either dramatically or quietly--Kicker or Soft-shoe tap ending). The Lead is like some banner-bearing personage holding up a symbolic object. In a Christian service she/he is the crucifer carrying the Cross. The Build-up of the ritual poem is like the progression toward the altar. The climactic arrival at the altar can be marked by an ecclesiastical act -- perhaps an offering. Whitman uses this ecclesiastical ending for Section 5, "I give you my sprig of lilac." The lilac's 'heart-shaped leaves' connote love; the blossom, fertility and the miracle of birth, Allen and Davis explain.

Ritual is helpful to the mourner because it offers a way for her or him to appeal to faith for its meaning and hope in an unbearably emotional time. The ritual also suggests and thus legitimizes people's feelings about there being order in our existence because there is order in the Cosmos. The mourner can then accept the concept or belief that there is purpose for death and life, hence credibility for his or her existence and for that of the person or persons who have died.

Of course, one is simultaneously dealing with horrendous surges of emotions, but here is where the language of a poem like "When Lilacs Last in the Dooryard Bloom'd" can have a calming and meaningful role. With combinations of words about people and nature, Whitman provides pleasant and comfortable sounding lines of language that can be soothing and even hopeful in theological and philosophical ways. This is a function of the poetry of bereavement.

The section or stanza, of course, does not have to be in the form of a processional to be a ritual poem. In one of the ritual poems in "When Lilacs Last in the Dooryard Bloom'd," Whitman describes the farmhouse where he was born (still standing in West Hills, the Walt Whitman Birthplace State Historic Site and Interpretive Center administered by the Walt Whitman Birthplace Association):

In the dooryard fronting an old farm-house near the white-wash'd palings,
Stands the lilac-bush tall-growing with heart-shaped leaves of rich green,
With many a pointed blossom rising delicate, with the perfume strong I love,
With every leaf a miracle--and from this bush in the dooryard,
With delicate-color'd blossoms and heart-shaped leaves of rich green,
A sprig with its flower I break.

The purple-flowered lilacs were in full blossom that Good Friday in Washington, the casket later banked with these flowers, the strong sweet odor becoming the incense in "When Lilacs Last in the Dooryard Bloom'd." Whitman writes, "I find myself always reminded of the great tragedy of that day by the sight and odor of these blossoms."

"O how shall I warble myself for the dead there I loved?" Whitman's cry for the words to express his grief persists throughout the long poem.

"And how shall I deck my song for the large sweet soul that has gone?

"And what shall my perfume be for the grave of him I love?"

Whitman's is the cry of so many doing mourning, "Oh, I don't have the words to say how I feel!" cries the tear gushing victim. But the grieved can find the words in poetic language, in Whitman's "When Lilacs Last in the Dooryard Bloom'd."

O what shall I hang on the chamber walls?
And what shall the pictures be that I hang on the walls,
To adorn the burial-house of him I love?

Whitman's answer, the pictures he felt should adorn a democratic President's tomb:

Pictures of growing spring and farms and homes,
When the Fourth-month eve at sundown, and the gray smoke lucid and bright,
With floods of the yellow gold of the gorgeous, indolent, sinking sun, burning, expanding the air,
With the fresh sweet herbage under foot, and the pale green leaves of the trees prolific,
In the distance the flowing glaze, the breast of the river, with a wind-dapple here and there,
With ranging hills on the banks, with many a line against the sky, and shadows,
And the city at hand with dwellings so dense, and stacks of chimneys,
And all the scenes of life and the workshops, and the workmen homeward returning.

With these pictures he surrounds his adoration of Abraham Lincoln. Whitman thinks of rural and urban memories that in a poem of bereavement are meaningful for him. He thinks about the spectacular Paumanok sunsets, the brush and trees, and uses these to express his love for Earth's beauty as a way of bearing the grief that overwhelms him. He thinks about the city scenes and people carrying on their ordinary lives that he observed as a reporter and editor of several New York City newspapers. This love of his for the people is a comfort to him in his grief for the President who also felt love for the people.

If you write a longer poem consider including a refrain which Whitman does with the song of the Hermit Thrush, "the grand climax of all bird music," asserts F. Schuyler Matthews in his 1904 classic <u>Field Book of Birds and Their Music</u>. "The song," claims Matthews' contemporary, the naturalist essayist John Burroughs, "suggests a serene, religious beatitude as no other sound in nature does." Whitman himself says the

Hermit Thrush's song is "the sweetest, solemnest of all our singing birds," a statement suggesting that he actually heard the bird and this would have had to be while walking the Long Island Pine Barrens which he pictures in his lines about the song. What Whitman heard, according to Eric Salzmann, music theater composer and ornithologist of Quogue and Brooklyn, in his article, "Sweet Singer of the Pine Barrens" (*Terra Nova: Nature & Culture*, Summer 1997), would have been song that "rises and falls in a long series of variations on a simple pattern ('varying ever-altering song'), starting with a low and 'pure deliberate note' and then bursting up 'liquid and free and tender' to a high warble or trill. The ascending tones are produced as two-note chords, giving a reedy effect. The song, typically delivered in the gathering dusk from a low perch inside the forest, is quite ventriloquial and far-carrying, seemingly amplified and enriched by the surrounding trees and the dense evening air." Salzmann asserts, "It is through the song of the bird and its continuity in the landscape that Whitman comes to terms with the death of Lincoln . . .." In his critical biography, <u>The Solitary Singer</u>, (Grove Press, New York, 1955), New York University Professor Gay Wilson Allen says "the burden of the hermit thrush's song is the necessity of death in the natural process."

In the swamp, in secluded recesses
A shy and hidden bird is warbling a song.

Solitary the thrush,
The hermit withdrawn to himself, avoiding the settlements,
Sings by himself a song.

Song of the bleeding throat!
Death's outlet song of life, (for well dear brother I know,
If thou wast not granted to sing thou wouldst surely die).

Again, later in the poem in different words:

Sing on, sing on you gray-brown bird,
Sing from the swamps, the recesses, pour your chant from the bushes,
Limitless out of the dusk, out of the cedars and pines.

Sing on dearest brother, warble your reedy song,
Loud human song, with voice of uttermost woe.

O liquid and free and tender!
O wild and loose to my soul—O wondrous singer!
You only I hear—yet the star holds me, (but will soon depart,)
Yet the lilac with mastering odor holds me.

bios

Dr. David B. Axelrod shares the Whitman legacy now as Suffolk County Poet Laureate. His newest of seventeen books, The Impossibility of Dreams, was just published by AhadadaBooks (Tokyo and Toronto, 2007). He is recipient of three Fulbright Awards and a frequent performer and workshop teacher. Dr. Axelrod maintains a website at www.poetrydoctor.org

~

Edgar Carlson is a native Long Islander. He lives in Farmingdale and owns a landscape-gardening company. He is an MFA student at Adelphi University. Last year he created a 2007 Poetry & Art Calendar published by Allbook Books. He has three grandchildren.

~

Vince Clemente, a SUNY English Professor Emeritus, is a poet-biographer, whose books include John Ciardi: Measure of the Man (Univ. of Arkansas Press); Paumanok Rising: Long Island Figures in a Landscape; and seven volumes of verse. For many years a trustee of the Walt Whitman Birthplace and founding editor of *West Hills Review: A Walt Whitman Journal*, he is presently a columnist for *The Sag Harbor Express* and Consulting Editor, America, for *The Seventh Quarry: Swansea Poetry Magazine*. *The Vince Clemente Papers* are now part of the Rush Rhees Library of Rochester University, *The Vince Clemente Journals & Memorabilia* with Smithtown Library's Long Island Room.

~

Jonathan Cohen, a poet, translator, and independent scholar, has translated the work of several major Latin American poets, including Ernesto Cardenal, Enrique Lihn, Roque Dalton, Octavio Paz, and Pedro Mir. His translation of Cardenal's From Nicaragua, With Love: Poems, 1979-1986 (1987) won the Robert Payne Award of the Translation Center at Columbia University. He is editing a new collection of Cardenal's poetry, to be titled Pluriverse: New and Selected Poems, forthcoming from New Directions in 2008. His recent book, A Pan-American Life: Selected Poetry and Prose of Muna Lee (2004), recovers the work of Muna Lee, a prominent poet and social activist.

~

Gary Corseri writes, "Revolution without the Arts is meaningless." He endeavors "to humanize and aestheticize political-social-economic consciousness and to revolutionize and socialize the perspectives of artists." His articles, poems, stories and plays have appeared at *The New York Times, Cyrano'sJournalOnline, ThomasPaine'sCorner, The Village Voice, Georgia Review, City Lights Review, CounterPunch, CommonDreams, WorldProutAssembly, PalestineChronicle, TelesurTV.net*, and 200 others. Born and raised in New York City, Gary has taught in public schools, prisons and universities. He currently resides in the D.C. area, with his wife, the writer Yoko Kagawa.

~

Mark Donnelly's poetry has been published in *Long Island Quarterly, Missing Spoke Press, Minimus 2000* and *96inc*. He has also had short stories and dramatic monologues published. He holds an MFA in Creative Writing from Brooklyn College.

~

Sasha Ettinger is a retired Special Education teacher. For several years, she has participated in Max Wheat's Taproot Workshops and George Wallace's Hutton House workshops. She is a founding member of the Poets Circle at the Graphic Eye Gallery in Port Washington. Her poetry will appear in the upcoming anthology, Songs of Seasoned Women edited by Patti Tana.

~

Darrel Blaine Ford is my real name, although when young I often used the name Velsor Brush (one of Whitman's early noms de plume). I first bicycled to his birthplace in West Hills, Long Island, NY when I was nine-years old in 1939. My way of celebrating Walt Whitman is to personate him, wearing the dented brown slouch hat and careless 19th century garb. I tell his story in the first person and read his poetry as he did to school children, to library and club groups, and to college audiences. E-mail: waltwhitmanofli@aol.com or phone me: (631) 661-7040.

~

Jean Franco has taught at the Universities of Essex, London, Stanford and Columbia and is now Professor Emerita. Her articles and books on Latin American culture include Plotting Women: Gender and Representation in Mexico (Columbia University Press, 1989); The Decline and Fall of the Lettered City: Latin America and the Cold War (Harvard University Press, 2000). A collection of essays, Critical Passions was published by Duke University Press (1999). The most recent publication is the essay, "Rape: A Weapon of War," (June 2007). In 2006, she was awarded the Aguila Azteca by the Mexican government in recognition of her contribution to the study of Mexican culture.

~

Ray Freed's poems have appeared in journals and periodicals in the US, Canada, and Britain. Books and chapbooks include Sea Animal On Land, 1970; Necessary Lies, 1975; Shinnecock Bay, 1977; Much Cry Little Wool, 1990; Hualalai, 1995; The Juggler's Ball, 1996; and All Horses Are Flowers, 1998. He has given numerous public and private readings of his work, and in Spring 1990 served as Poet-in-Residence at the State University of New York at Stony Brook. He lives in Kona on the Big Island of Hawaii.

~

Geraldine Green's first collection The Skin, was published 2003, and her second collection Passio was published 2005, both by Flarestack. Her work has been published in the US, UK and Italy and she has read widely in these countries; currently undertaking a PhD (Creative Writing) at Lancaster University, Geraldine is fresh from performing at the first International Women's Arts Festival in the UK. She runs poetry workshops, teaches creative writing at Lancaster University, is an Associate Editor of *Poetry Bay* www.poetrybay.com, (editor NYC poet George Wallace), lives in Cumbria, UK and is working on her third collection.

~

Mankh (Walter E. Harris III) is a regular poet (whatever that means), haiku poet, essayist, small press publisher, and Turtle Islander. His poems and essays have been published in various Long Island venues as well as online at *voidmagazine.com*, *performancepoets.org*, *poetryvlog.com*, *Thomas Paine's Corner/Cyrano's Journal Online*, *Creations Magazine*, and others. He is an associate editor of *Long Island Quarterly*. Nature, music, current events, various cultural traditions and spiritual pathways all feed his creativity. Mankh's poem "My God has an O" was nominated for a Pushcart Prize.

~

Gladys Henderson is an artist, poet, teacher and retired retail executive. An award-winning poet, most recently she was a finalist for the Paumanok Poetry Award 2006. She leads a weekly poetry workshop at the Graphic Eye Gallery in Port Washington, New York and conducts the monthly poetry critique for Live Poets, Islip, NY.

~

Evelyn Kandel is a visual artist who began, in the 1990s, to include poems in her artwork. Since then she has concentrated on writing poetry. She is a member of Taproot with Maxwell Wheat and Poets' Circle with Gladys Henderson. She has studied poetry at C.W. Post and with George Wallace. A hostess for Performance Poets Association[tm], she has also been a featured reader. Her poems have been published in *Lucidity*, *Long Island Quarterly*, *PPA Literary Reviews*, *Taproot*, and the anthology Long Island Sounds: 2007. Evelyn's work will also appear in the forthcoming anthology Songs of Seasoned Women.

~

Rita Katz is the author of five chapbooks of poetry. She was born in Brooklyn, New York and is the mother of two sons. She now resides in Port Washington, Long Island. In addition to writing poetry, she is a professional artist on the board of the Art Advisory Council of Port Washington. Her awards include the 1900 and 2000 MC Carten award from the Academy of American Poets, numerous honorable mentions-- 2007 from the Mid-Island Y JCC. Her poems will be appearing in two other anthologies in 2007. Her art is represented in the permanent collection at Nassau Community College in Garden City, Long Island.

~

Ann Kenna is a third generation Long Islander, student, teacher, wife, and mother. She works in Special Education and conducts a poetry workshop for students. She is a member of the Long Island Writers' Guild, Long Island Poetry Collective, The North Sea Poetry Scene, and the Farmingdale Poetry Group. She has been a featured poet in venues around the Metropolitan area. Her poetry can be found in *Meadowlark*, the summer 2007 Issue of *Oberon*, the September 2006 and March 2007 issues of *Flutter Poetry Journal*, and Long Island Sounds: 2007.

~

Jeanette Klimszewski, a graduate of New York University, thrived in a career as a Physical Education teacher and a coach for various high school varsity teams. Her specialty in archery and field hockey earned her local and state awards. After retirement from teaching, she attended Clown Camp at the University of Wisconsin-LaCrosse to become Klancy the Clown. She clowned at County Fairs, convalescent homes, and entertained abandoned and abused children. Entering Taproot, a writing program for seniors, she became active in local poetry projects. Mentored by peers, her work has appeared in poetry columns and periodicals. She is the author of <u>Promise</u> (Fore Angels Press).

~

Charlene Babb Knadle's poems, short stories, essays, and literary criticism have appeared in many publications, including the multi-volume library reference work, <u>Popular Contemporary Writers</u>. She has two poetry chapbooks: <u>Dandelion Sleeves</u>, <u>Local Color</u> (Two Cardinals Press) and a novel: <u>Paper Lovers</u>, by C.B. Knadle (Publish America). She is working on a memoir tentatively titled <u>My Year in Leavenworth</u>. Her 1998 doctorate is from St. John's University. She teaches in the SUNY system at Suffolk County Community College.

~

Norbert Krapf, who taught for 34 years at Long Island University and directed the C.W. Post Poetry Center, lives in Indianapolis. His latest book, from Indiana Univ. Pr., is a collaboration with photographer Darryl Jones, <u>Invisible Presence</u>. Acme Records will release his jazz and poetry collaboration with pianist and composer Monika Herzig, <u>Imagine: Indiana in Music and Words</u>, and his <u>New and Selected Indiana Poems</u> is forthcoming from IU Press.

~

Mindy Kronenberg's poetry has won awards and appeared in numerous publications in the US and abroad. Ms. Kronenberg frequently performs her work for BOCES and Poets & Writers and has appeared on various broadcast media. She is a mentor and Director of Academic Support at SUNY, Empire State College, edits *Book/Mark Quarterly Review*, facilitates the Writers Space in Babylon, and is a trustee for the Miller Place Historical Society.

~

Ali Lebow is a poet and an artist. She loves traveling, movies, and volleyball. She attends Trinity School in New York City, and loves to be with her friends. Ali's poems have been published in Haiku One Breaths and Modern Muses, the latter for which she also did the cover artwork. She became a bat mitzvah in June of 2004.

~

D. H. Melhem is the author of seven books of poetry, most recently New York Poems (Syracuse University Press, 2005), three novels, including Stigma & The Cave (Syracuse, 2007), a musical drama, a creative writing workbook, over 60 essays, and two anthologies. Her critical works on Black poets include the first comprehensive study of Gwendolyn Brooks. Among awards for poetry and prose: an American Book Award, a National Endowment for the Humanities Fellowship, three Pushcart Prize nominations, a CUNY Ph.D. Alumni Association Special Achievement Award, and a RAWI Lifetime Achievement Award (2007). Dr. Melhem serves as vice-president of the International Women's Writing Guild.

~

Pedro Mir (1913-2000) is the Dominican Republic's foremost literary figure of the 20th century. He originally published his *Countersong to Walt Whitman* in 1952. In 1947, the subject of mounting suspicions of the Trujillo dictatorship, Mir was forced to go into exile. When he returned fifteen years later, following the death of the dictator, the poet immediately won the hearts of the Dominican people, and his poetry recitals were mass public events attended by enthusiastic crowds of citizens from every walk of life. In 1982 the legislature of the Dominican Congress conferred upon Mir the title of National Poet, and in January 1993 he received the National Prize for Literature, the highest honor a literary artist can receive in the Dominican Republic.

~

Annabelle Moseley is Poet-in-Residence at The Stevenson Academy of Fine Arts in Oyster Bay, New York, where she teaches adult writing classes. She also teaches English and runs the Creative Writing Club at Saint Anthony's High School in South Huntington, NY. Her published chapbooks are The Moon Is A Lemon (Birnham Wood Graphics, 2005) and Artifacts of Sound (Street Press, 2007). Her poems have appeared or are forthcoming in such journals as *The Texas Review*, *The Seventh Quarry*,

The New Formalist, Mezzo Cammin, and *Soundings East.*

~

Tammy Nuzzo-Morgan is the founder and president of The North Sea Poetry Scene. She was a 2005 nominee for Poet Laureate of Suffolk County, NY and a 2006 nominee for a Pulitzer Prize for her poetry book, Let Me Tell You Something. She is listed in Poets & Writers. Her books also include: Between Willow and Cedars, The Bitter The Sweet, One Woman's Voice, For Michael, Howling The Moon. She is the Editor of Long Island Sounds Anthology. She is endeavoring to create an archival/arts center for Long Island poetry, website: http://www.lipoetryarchivalcenter.com
E-mail: Thenorthseapoetryscene@hotmail.com
Her website: http://groups.msn.com/PoetryofTammyNuzzoMorgan

~

Anthony Policano is a Long Island poet who began writing in college. A former technology manager for J.P. Morgan Chase, his passion for poetry has recently reawakened. He writes, attends workshops and reads his work publicly at every opportunity. In 2007, he was awarded 1st place in the Long Island Poetry Collective contest and received honorable mentions in several others. His poems have been published in *PPA Literary Review, Loomings, Flutter Poetry Journal, Poetryvlog.com,* and are to be published in *Xanadu,* Autumn 2007. Anthony is married, has a daughter, and calls Oyster Bay home.

~

Christina M. Rau is the founder of Poets In Nassau and has been a poet all her life give or take a few of the beginning years. Because poetry doesn't pay, she teaches yoga, aerobics, college English, and manners for money. Her novel is currently being rejected by a myriad of publishers, but her poetry has appeared in the 2007 issues of *Blue Fog Journal* and *The Verse Marauder,* and she placed first in the Performance Poets Association[tm] annual contest. She loves moonbeams and puppies. And sarcasm.

~

Ruth Sabath Rosenthal is a NY poet, published in literary journals and anthologies: *The Aurorean, Birmingham Poetry Review, Connecticut Review, Creations Magazine, Chronogram, Ibbetson Street, Jabberwock Review, Long Island Quarterly, MÖBIUS The Poetry Magazine, Pacific Review, Poetica, Poetry Depth Quarterly, Voices Israel 2007 - Vol. 33*, and <u>Songs of Seasoned Women</u>. On October 15th (Ruth's birthday) in 2006, her poem "on yet another birthday" was nominated for a Pushcart Prize by Ibbetson Street.

~

Andrea Rowen is a poet whose real-world poetry is informed by wisdom traditions of both the East and West. With a BA in Writing and Literature and seminary certification in Biblical Exegesis, Andrea joins the spiritual experience to the deep Romanticism of the Transcendentalists and the wildness of the Beats. A Long Island native, Andrea's years abroad have given her a worldview that helps dissect the apparent into subtle realities rendering them into a refined "poetry of understanding." Her upcoming project, "New Hymns For The Promised Land," will feature a small collection of poetry performed to original bass guitar compositions.

~

Richard Savadsky is a poet, artist, and retired engineer, as well as a lover of humanity, the animal kingdom, and the universe. He was born in Brooklyn on February 28, 1942. He graduated from Polytechnic Institute of Brooklyn, with a BS in Aerospace Engineering, and earned his MBA at Adelphi University. He worked for the US Navy, 1963-64, in Patuxent River, Maryland, and served in the Army, 1964-66. Richard worked for Grumman Aerospace Corporation and Grumman International for over twenty years. He is a staff member of Performance Poets Association[tm], and the author of <u>Endorphin Brigade: Fruits, Vegetables and My Journey With MS</u>.

~

Robert Savino is a native Long Island poet. His poems have been published widely, in print, from *Long Island Quarterly* to *The Haight Ashbury Literary Journal*, as well as in <u>The Light of City and Sea: an Anthology of Suffolk County Poetry, 2006</u> (Street Press); and online in *PoetrySuperHighway, Combat,* and *http://poetry.about.com*. Robert was a recent winner of the Lake Ronkonkoma Historical Society's poetry competition, and a long-standing Board Member of Island Poets.

~

Alan Semerdjian is a poet/songwriter/artist/english teacher with lots of work out there in the world including a chapbook through Lock N Load Press (2005) and a full-length collection of poems (due out 2007) through Spuyten Duyvil. His digital home is www.alanarts.com, and more about his music is found at: www.alansemerdjian.com

~

Genevieve Shore, born and raised in New York City, still feels the life of the city in her bones. She holds a BA in Psychology from New York University and spent most of her 30 years in advertising at Waring & LaRosa, rising to SVP, Account Director. Recently, she started writing poetry, with its infinite possibilities of nuance and meaning. Her favorite poets include Walt Whitman, Wallace Stevens and Dylan Thomas, all for their sense of the mystical. Gen is working on Sea Chronicles, a collection of poems, and lives with her husband in Connecticut and Florida.

~

Barbara Southard lives and works in Miller Place, NY. Her poems have been published in *Poet Lore, Long Island Quarterly, Home Planet News, The Long-Islander, Journal For Living*, and several anthologies, including <u>Long Island Sounds 2005, 2006, 2007</u> (The North Sea Poetry Scene Press), and <u>For Loving Precious Beast</u> (Purple Sage Press). Currently, she is a board member of the Long Island Poetry Collective, conducts a writing workshop in Wyandanch Library for Babylon Arts Council, and co-facilitates a poetry discussion group at Half Hollow Hills Library in Dix Hills.

~

Douglas G. Swezey, a resident of East Northport, has been writing poetry since high school. He received his BA in English and Art History from Stony Brook University in 2004. He has worked at the Walt Whitman Birthplace State Historic Site and Interpretive Center and written as a journalist for many weekly newspapers. He is the author of <u>Stony Brook University: Off The Record</u> (College Prowler, 2005), and currently serves as Treasurer on the Board of the Long Island Poetry Collective. His poetry can be found in <u>Long Island Sounds: 2007</u>.

~

J R (Judy) Turek is in her tenth year as Moderator of the Farmingdale Creative Writing Group. She is Secretary of The North Sea Poetry Scene, and the author of They Come and They Go (Long Island Expressions). She strives to write a poem-a-day and mostly succeeds. In 2007, she was a co-editor of Long Island Sounds: 2007, Finding Our Voices, and PPA Literary Review #11. A born-and-bred Long Islander, J R resides in East Meadow with her soul-mate husband, her dogs, and her extensive shoe collection. If you see the license plate MSJEVUS, follow her; chances are, she's going to a poetry event.

~

Pramila Venkateswaran, author of Thirtha, published by Yuganta Press, has poems in *Paterson Literary Review*, *Ariel*, *Atlanta Review*, *Prairie Schooner*, *Kavya Bharati*, and *Calyx*, as well as anthologies, including A Chorus for Peace and En(Compass). She has performed her poems nationally, most recently at the Geraldine R. Dodge Poetry Festival. She teaches English and women's studies at Nassau Community College, NY.

~

George Wallace is author of fourteen chapbooks and two CDs of poetry, editor of *Poetrybay*, *Poetryvlog*, *Polarity*, and a performing artist who has appeared on stage at such venues as Howlfest (NY), Woody Guthrie Festival (Oklahoma), the Beat Museum (San Francisco) and Dylan Thomas Centre (Wales). A former member of the Board of Directors of the Walt Whitman Birthplace, in 2003 he was named first Poet Laureate for Suffolk County, NY.

~

Muriel Harris Weinstein has two books coming out in 2008: When Louis Armstrong Taught Me Scat from Chronicle Books, and Play Louie, Play! Louis Armstrong's biography, from Bloomsbury Books, a British/American publisher. She also has work in the forthcoming anthology Songs of Seasoned Women edited by Patti Tana. This year she won the Nassau Review Poetry Award for 2007, first place in the Performance Poets Association[tm] contest, and second place in the Mid-Island Y JCC competition. Her work has appeared in *The Comstock Review*, *Outerbridge*, *Jewish Currents*, *Cape Rock*, and *Voices International*.

~

Maxwell Corydon Wheat, Jr. was appointed, by poets, Nassau County's first Poet Laureate, on June 24, 2007, at a ceremony on the grounds of Cedarmere, the Roslyn Harbor home of the 19th Century poet, William Cullen Bryant. Wheat is a volunteer for programing at Cedarmere, a Nassau County historic site. He has been a member of the Board of Trustees of the Walt Whitman Birthplace Association, serving as program chairperson and director of the annual children's poetry contest where he developed a teacher's guide for encouraging more use of details by young poets.

~

Martin Willitts, Jr. is a Senior Librarian in New York. He has recent publications in *Pebble Lake Review*, Hurricane Blues (anthology), *Hotmetalpress.net*, *Haigaonline*, *Bent Pin*, *5th Gear*, and others. He has a fifth chapbook Falling In and Out of Love (Pudding House Publications, 2005), an online chapbook Farewell, the journey being taken (www.languageandculture.net in 2006), a full length book of poems with his art The Secret Language of the Universe (March Street Press, 2006), and another chapbook Lowering the Nets of Light, forthcoming from Pudding House Publications.

~

Ernie Wormwood has been published in *The Antietam Review*, *Rhino*, *Perpetuum Mobile*, *Main Channel Voices*, *Creation Journal*, *The Broadkill Review*, and at *Innisfree Poetry*, *Hotmetal Press*, and *ArabesquesPress* online. She was recently featured in Grace Cavalieri's "The Poet and the Poem" broadcast for the Library of Congress. Her book reviews appear in *The Montserrat Review*. She is grateful to the Squaw Valley Community of Writers and Stony Brook/Southampton Writer's Conference for artistic support. A Washington, D.C. native, Ernie lives in Leonardtown, Maryland. She may be reached at: erniewormwood@md.metrocast.net

~

Bill Zavatsky has taught at the Trinity School in Manhattan for the past twenty years. His most recent book of poems is Where X Marks the Spot (Hanging Loose Press, 2006). Translations will appear in Essential Poems and Writing of Robert Desnos (Black Widow Books). His and Ron Padgett's new edition of The Poems of A. O. Barnabooth by Valery Larbaud will be republished (also by Black Widow) in 2008. His work has been anthologized in Up Late and The Face of Poetry, and he has written poems as liner notes for CDs by jazz pianist Marc Copland.

~

acknowledgments - *the following were first published...*

"Preface for Walt Whitman" by D.H. Melhem, <u>Country: An Organic Poem</u> (Merrick, NY: Cross-Cultural Communications, 1998).

"Walt" by Geraldine Green, at *poetryvlog.com*

"Foreword to the *Countersong*" by Jean Franco and excerpts from *Countersong to Walt Whitman* by Pedro Mir, translated by Jonathan Cohen, Washington: Azul Editions, 2006 <www.azuleditions.com>

"Whitman Recidivist" by Gary Corseri, *Calamus*.

"Go Like Whitman" by George Wallace, <u>Long Island Sounds: 2007 An Anthology of Poetry From Maspeth to Montauk And Beyond</u> (The North Sea Poetry Scene Press).

"Visiting With Walt" by Jeanette Klimszewski, *The Long-Islander*, 1997. The poem herein has been slightly revised.

"Looking for Walt Whitman at C.W. Post" herein slightly revised, and "Walt Whitman's Daughters" appeared at: <www.cwpost.liu.edu/cwis/cwp/50th_poetry.html> as part of Campus Meditations (© 2004 Norbert Krapf), a poem cycle written to celebrate the 50th anniversary of the C.W. Post Campus of Long Island University.

"*O how shall I warble myself for the dead one I loved?*" by Maxwell Corydon Wheat, Jr., *Bird Watcher's Digest*, March/April 1992 issue.

"Beyond the palisade" by Ann Kenna, *Flutter Poetry Journal* online at <http://www.freewebs.com/rarepetal/index.htm> Vol 1, Issue 4, September 2006. The poem herein has been slightly revised.

"Flying Island" by Richard Savadsky, <u>Endorphin Brigade: Fruits, Vegetables and My Journey with MS</u> (Allbook Books, 2006).

"Into the Light: Safe Haven 1944" by Ruth Sabath Rosenthal, *Poetica*, March 2007 issue.

"Walt Whitman's Natural Resources" by Maxwell Corydon Wheat, Jr., *Nature Study* - Summer 1969. The excerpt herein has been slightly revised.

"Poets to Come: Teaching Whitman in High School" by Bill Zavatsky, in <u>The Teachers and Writers Guide to Walt Whitman</u> (Teachers and Writers Collaborative) and in <u>The Teachers and Writers Guide to Classic American Literature</u> (Teachers and Writers Collaborative). The excerpt herein has been slightly revised.

other books available from Allbook Books

IF YOU SEE MY DOG, THE NAME IS MOON (2007) poems by Pierre Gazarian
$11 postage paid
ECSTATIC (2007) poems by Mira McEwan $11ppd / list price $11.95
ENDORPHIN BRIGADE: Fruits, Vegetables and My Journey with MS (2006)
(Multiple Sclerosis) - poems by Richard Savadsky - humorous and personal
$11ppd / list price $11
2007 Poetry & Art Calendar - Edgar Carlson and David C. Hartrick
poem and artwork with each month $5ppd

written/edited by Mankh (Walter E. Harris III)
MODERN MUSES: How Artists Become Inspired (2005)
anthology of essays, poems, photos, and more
168 pgs. - $15 ppd / list price $15
HAIKU ONE BREATHS: a voice through a tangle (2004)
how-to haiku, plus poems from 22 other poets, and Chinese calligraphy
160 pgs. - $13 ppd / list price $13
SINGING AN EPIC OF PEACE: a Fifth World Story-Poem
Appliable to Worlds Both Inner and Outer (2003)
(262 pgs. including Chinese calligraphy and introductory notes)
$15 ppd / list price $17

Chapbooks:
Poetry Series: $6 each ppd / $20 for all 4.
(#1) SPIRAL of LIFE: journeys, nature and friends (35 pages of poetry)
(#2) PRESENCE of BIRDS (34 pgs. including 11 pgs. of haiku)
(#3) A NET for the MOON (27 pgs. of poetry)
(#4) AROMAS FINER THAN PRAYER (39 pgs. of poetry)

NATURAL PEREGRINATIONS - a holistic monograph by Buffalo (tou tovxa) $6 ppd

*

N.Y. State residents -- tax is included.
Elsewhere in the U.S.A. -- no tax.
Please make check or money order payable to: *Allbook Books*

For multiple or special orders, or outside the USA, please contact for prices.

For information regarding books, poetry readings, tutorials, apprenticeship, haiku workshops, learning the art of Chinese calligraphy, text and graphic layout services for publishing, or, for further information please write to >

W.E. Harris III
Allbook Books
P.O. Box 562
Selden, NY 11784

e-mail: **mankh@allbook-books.com**
website: **www.allbook-books.com**

*O setting sun! though the time has come,
I still warble under you, if none else does, unmitigated adoration.*

~ Walt Whitman
from "Song at Sunset"